Also by Lyndsay Green

Teens Gone Wired: Are You Ready?
You Could Live a Long Time: Are You Ready?
The Perfect Home for a Long Life: Choosing the Right
Retirement Lifestyle for You

Ready to Retire?

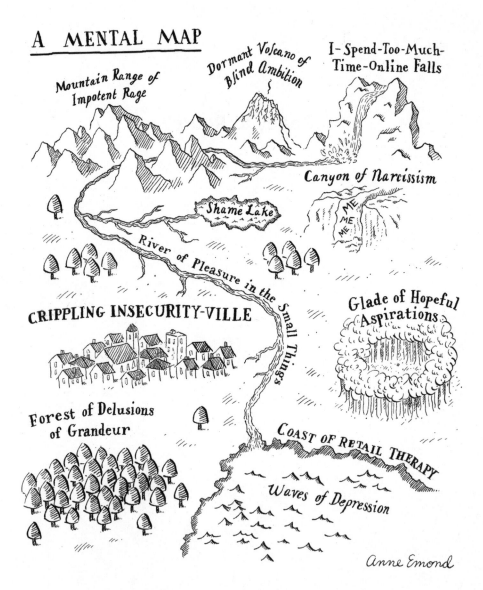

Ready to Retire?

The New Reality of Retirement and
What You and Your Spouse Need to Know

LYNDSAY GREEN

Patrick Crean Editions
HarperCollins Publishers Ltd

Ready to Retire?
Copyright © 2016 by Lyndsay Green.
All rights reserved.

Published by Patrick Crean Editions, an imprint of HarperCollins Publishers Ltd

First edition

No part of this book may be used or reproduced in any manner whatsoever without the prior written permission of the publisher, except in the case of brief quotations embodied in reviews.

HarperCollins books may be purchased for educational, business, or sales promotional use through our Special Markets Department.

HarperCollins Publishers Ltd
2 Bloor Street East, 20th Floor
Toronto, Ontario, Canada
M4W 1A8

www.harpercollins.ca

Library and Archives Canada Cataloguing in Publication information is available upon request.

Map illustration by Anne Emond

ISBN 978-1-44344-056-1

Printed and bound in the United States of America
RRD 9 8 7 6 5 4 3 2 1

For Hank, my very own retiree

Contents

—·•·—

Ready to Retire?

Men and Retirement

When I told a retirement-aged man that I was working on a book about men's retirement, he replied, "Ah, you're writing about death." His quip made us both laugh, but the response was more than glib cocktail banter. My research had been uncovering the sense of impending doom that can accompany discussions of retirement. A schoolteacher told me the following story to prepare me for some of the attitudes I would encounter. He had attended a pre-retirement seminar provided by his employer, and the instructor started with the following quiz. "When you retire you need to be prepared for the three Ds. Name them." At this point in his story, the teacher asked *me* to fill in the blanks. All I could think of were non-D words like *liberation, leisure, reinvention.* I finally came up with *dishes*—making the assumption a retiree wasn't used to pulling his weight at home. The D words he was looking for were *drink, depression* and *divorce.* And now my jester had given me a fourth D to add—*death.*

I was trying to understand men's retirement because I could see it was going to be a critical stage in the lives of the men I love—my husband, my brothers and my friends who were quickly closing in on 65. Having spent the past decade researching aging, I have seen the way our assumptions and expectations cloud reality. I found the gap between myth and reality to be particularly wide for the period of aging we have labelled *retirement*, especially when it comes to men. Given the captivating images that accompanied those "Freedom 55" television ads that ran in the 1980s, I assumed that men were chomping at the bit to sever their work chains to be free to run along the beach, roar around in their convertibles and hit the golf course. Instead, I found a great fear of retirement. Most of the male seniors I interviewed for *You Could Live a Long Time: Are You Ready?* advised me to forget about retiring and urged me to develop a work plan rather than a retirement plan. One of them warned me that if I stopped working I'd age rapidly, just as the people of Shangri-La did when they left their isolated mountain paradise in James Hilton's book *Lost Horizon*. He told me some of his colleagues couldn't wait to retire, and then went into decline as soon as they did.

But I also had the experience of my father to consider. He retired just before his 65th birthday after negotiating a satisfactory pension with his employer, the federal government, and left on mutually agreeable terms. He had worked hard throughout his career in both the private and public sectors, and had made a real contribution. When it was over, he walked out the door and never looked back. He lived another twenty-five years, and I don't remember him ever saying that he missed his work. If he found retirement distressing, he never let on.

What I saw was a man who couldn't wait to get up in the morning and tackle his "to-do" list. He was a civil engineer with an MBA who had worked in the oil and gas sector, and his retirement projects exercised all the skills he had accumulated. He had a steady stream of home renovation projects on the go and carried them out with obsessive precision. He tracked his investments religiously on elaborate spread sheets and used the output to mail his three children well-argued financial strategies. He maintained his professional interest in the vagaries of fossil fuels and sent us tips on switching our furnaces from oil to gas, or vice versa, and safety tips on the use of propane.

Genealogy became a passion, and we received meticulously researched family histories, sometimes in response to a request from a grandchild doing a class project. A visit from any of his seven grandchildren was the cause for an exhaustive tour of the local tourist hot spots, following to the letter a custom-prepared itinerary, often detailed down to the last quarter-hour. During family gatherings on frigid winter days, it was my father who hauled the visiting grandchildren out on the slopes to make sure they learned how to ski.

Another responsibility he took seriously was making his views known on the issues of the day—from submitting a twelve-page review of retirement pensions and savings plans to his Member of Parliament, to detailing the impact of a road-widening to his municipal councillor. And through all this, he kept up a personal regime of rigorous daily walking.

He was a busy guy. This was, no doubt, one of the reasons that my mother adapted pretty well to his retirement. That, and the fact that he continued to leave every morning for work—by walking downstairs to his basement office. It must be said that my mother was tormented by the length of time it took Dad to complete his home renovation projects. But there were few other major complaints, and my parents adjusted well to retirement—until the late-in-life arrival of another D word, *dementia*, that affected both of them.

But I wondered whether my father's experience would bear any resemblance to the retirements of the boomer men like my husband, my brothers and my friends. For one thing, there are so many of them. As the huge baby boom demographic ages, men are retiring in unprecedented numbers. The transition from work to non-work is occurring across a broad age spectrum with some people leaving the workforce before age 65 and others continuing to work well past 65. At the time of the last Canadian census, over 1.7 million men were aged 60 to 69, and this group is merely the leading edge of the demographic bulge.[1] Boomers as a generation are entering retirement healthier and with more resources than their predecessors, and with possibly a quarter to a third of their lives ahead of them. They're used to throwing their weight around and trying to change the political, social and cultural environments to suit their needs. The expectation is that this generation will reinvent and "retire" the old concept of retirement.

So *retirement* has become a bit of a dirty word, and the retirement industry, seminar leaders and authors struggle to come up with new labels to avoid the negative connotations. The euphemisms abound such as the Third Age, the Third Act and the Third Quarter. CARP and AARP, the national organizations that speak for retirees, used to be proudly known as the Canadian Association of Retired People and the American Association of Retired People, respectively. Now they rely on their acronyms with no reference to the words that used to underlie them.

Those "Freedom 55" ads introduced men to one version of the new retirement. When I canvassed my friends for their memories of these ads, we recall them setting the bar very high. We pictured a gorgeous buff man, who appeared to be a 35-year-old model with his hair dyed grey, lying on the beach next to an equally attractive and similarly contrived woman. We thought we had watched him beat some youngsters in a rousing game of beach volleyball. At least that was the vitality he exuded. If we were to add the current pressure for reinvention to the storyline, our hero would rinse the sand off his sculpted body and head off to a meeting about the new business he has started that will both make money and save the world. Not long after the Freedom 55 advertisement flooded TV channels, a weakened economy eroded retirement savings and comedians revised the slogan to "Freedom 95."

Negative stereotypes and contradictory cultural messages add to the complexity of the retirement picture presented to men. We say someone has been "put out to pasture" or "eased out the door." We are told, "You can't teach an old dog new tricks," and "After retirement life is a downhill slide." When I asked a friend how he and his buddies describe retirement he said, "There are *is*'s and *was*'s and now I'm a *was*." When we hear the phrase "old man," it's often coupled with the adjective "grumpy." Men are warned that they will become their fathers—for better or worse. Then there are the difficulties facing retired men on the home front. The one-liners abound: "A retired husband is often a wife's full-time job." "With retirement you get twice as much husband for half the income." "I married you for life but not for lunch."

And men are facing retirement at a time when other parts of their lives are changing. They may no longer be able to beat their younger partners at squash and need to work harder at keeping in shape. They may have more significant health challenges. Sexual performance is changing, and it may alter their interest in intimacy. They might be supporting elderly parents, unwell partners, adult children who are finding it hard to launch, and/or young late-in-life families. They may have become grandparents. Alternatively, they may find themselves alone.

These physical, psychological and social changes are taking place in an era when the very concept of what it is to be a man is under attack. Bestselling books have the titles *Are Men Necessary?* and *The End of Men.* The Munk Debates, the public policy forum that focuses on urgent global issues, chose "Are Men Obsolete?" as its topic in 2013. The resolution was: "Be it resolved: men are obsolete." Before the debate, 82 per cent of the audience voted against the resolution. After the debate, this number dropped to 56 per cent. So 44 per cent of those who heard the discussion agreed that men are now obsolete.

I wondered what the impact of this charged atmosphere was on my nearest and dearest, and all the other retirement-aged men out there. Although I'd grown up with two brothers and a very present father, and I've lived with the same man for the past four decades, I must admit that I didn't know men very well. Growing up as a young feminist, I had focused almost exclusively on women's issues, women writers and women's culture, and this bias was further reinforced by raising two daughters. I guess, if I'd thought about it, I would have said that the dominant culture was male, so by default I understood men. I found a very apt description of my attitude in Gail Sheehy's book *Understanding Men's Passages: Discovering the New Map of Men's Lives.* Sheehy has been chronicling social trends for both sexes for decades and this book was the first time she'd singled out men. She says she "faced a humbling admission: Men don't understand women, but at least they know it. Women don't understand men, but they *don't* know it."[2] Sheehy says we presume that we know what's wrong with our men and they could fix it if only they would listen to us. "But do many women really know what it's like for a man today?" she asks.[3]

So to figure out how our men are doing with retirement, I would need to set aside my stereotypes and preconceptions. And I would need to get men to tell me what they were *really* thinking about their lives at this stage. Clinging to my biases, I assumed this would not be easy. After all, didn't men have difficulty talking about their emotions? And, since men are from Mars and women are from Venus, would I be able to understand them even if they did speak candidly? In what became an eye-opening voyage, I was to discover that this stereotype, and so many others, just didn't hold up.

Background

When I began my research, I read that 30 per cent of men have difficulty adjusting to retirement.[4] Since over 1.7 million Canadian men are of retirement age, this means that hundreds of thousands of men are struggling, or soon will be struggling, with this stage of life. I wanted to understand the nature of these difficulties and their source. I was particularly interested in what effect our culture's stereotypes about retirement had on men, and how those stereotypes reconciled with research findings and men's own experiences. I was curious about how the messaging in literature and popular culture that shaped this generation's ideas of retirement was playing out in men's lives.

To understand these issues, analyzing the research findings was critical, but it wouldn't be enough. I needed to talk to men about their retirement. But I was warned that getting men to discuss an issue that pushed so many anxiety buttons wasn't going to be easy. As one man told me, "I've hung out with the same group of guys for years and we haven't really talked about most of these things you want to pry out of us." When Gail Sheehy was doing her research for *Understanding Men's Passages*, she asked men if they ever talk with other men about issues such as their pre-retirement anxiety, their concerns about aging, and "the whole question of potency in all areas of their lives." They almost always said no and gave the explanation, "It's a guy thing." Most of the time they didn't even discuss these matters with their wives.[5]

So I wasn't certain men would be open to having a frank discussion about retirement with me. As it turned out, my assumption was wrong. Once people were assured that the interview would be confidential, not only did virtually everyone I approached agree to be interviewed, several men sent me a message requesting an interview. From my book-writing experience, it was a first to have people asking to be subjected to an invasive interview.

After people agreed, I sent them the questionnaire I would be using as my interview guide. I felt it only fair to warn them my questions would be probing and intrusive, and I hoped they would give the questions some thought before we met. One man retracted his agreement to be interviewed after receiving the questionnaire and realizing how intimate the discussion would become. I felt relieved and grateful, as well as pleasantly surprised, that more people didn't bail out at this point. After all, I was asking them about their fears, and their fathers, and how they saw their futures. I wanted to know whether they were in control of the timing of their retirement and what role money played. I was inquiring about their relationships with their partners and their families, and the impact retirement might have on them. It doesn't get more personal than this.

Not only were men willing to talk, they approached the project with great candour and generosity of spirit. They talked about disappointments with themselves and family members, struggles that required counselling and treatment, fears about loss of status and respect. They also talked about the rewards of this stage of life, as well as the unexpected joys. They even talked about sex. I upped the ante by asking many of them to permit me to talk separately to their partners about their retirement, in interviews that would be confidential, even from them. Only one man declined that additional imposition.

The men and the women I interviewed told me that thinking about retirement had been a valuable exercise. One man said that if he'd gone through this interview process before he'd retired he would have done things differently. When I sent the interview guideline to spouses, they often discussed the questions with their husbands before meeting with me. They weren't certain of the answers to some of the questions I was asking about their spouses, questions such as who was his retirement role model, what he thought about his father's retirement and how he saw his life path.

The book includes insights from over sixty people—a combination of forty-four men and seventeen of their partners. They live in cities, small towns and rural areas across Canada. They range in age from 56 to 88 with two-thirds of them at peak retirement age, between 64 and 75. The people I interviewed cover the retirement spectrum. Some of them retired in their 50s, and some are still working in their 80s. Some left work happily, some unhappily. Some retired and then went back to work. Some are working and wish they weren't, and others wish they were still working. I interviewed men across a range of income levels, from low to high, including men at each level who felt they had saved enough for retirement, and those who had not. The group included men who were married, divorced and widowed, as well as men in common-law relationships, both heterosexual and homosexual. Having said that, this group could never be defined as representative of all men of retirement age. The purpose of their real-life stories is to add dimensions to the research findings and give the reader some flesh and blood examples.

I promised I would disguise the identities of the men and women I interviewed in order not to embarrass them or their families. In cases where the men are still working, I don't want to jeopardize their employment. As one man said, "I don't want my employer to find out that I want to retire by reading it in your book." So I've changed people's names, been vague about their occupations and disguised family details. My semi-retired husband was one of my interviewees, and I gave him a pseudonym as well, to ensure him a measure of privacy.

In my previous books, although I disguised people's identities, I listed their real names in the acknowledgements in order to thank them. For this book, because of the extreme sensitivity of many of the quotations, I have decided not to disclose anyone's identity. I am indebted to the interviewees for giving me the gift of their experiences. Thanks to them, the book has a rich tapestry of lives lived that gives substance to the book's research findings.

This is not a book about how to retire, when to retire or even whether men should retire. With all the messages and competing demands barraging men, I figure the last thing men need is more instruction on how to live their lives. Rather, the book is a description of what it is to be a retirement-aged man, so that these men, and the rest of us, can have a better appreciation of what they're going through. And it turns out that what most of them are experiencing is not the famous four Ds of drink, depression, divorce and death. Nor do the assumptions hold true that "Old dogs can't learn new tricks" and "Age must turn men into grumpy old men." Instead, while retirement has its challenges for men, and this period of life is complex and full of change, along with change comes opportunity. Most men are using the opportunity of retirement to follow unexplored routes or revisit neglected paths, to sharpen old skills or develop new ones, and to deepen their relationships, both with themselves and with others.

But men's fears about retirement are very real, and they can interfere with personal change and growth. The fears come from many sources: society's subtle and not so subtle messages, powerful works of art, concerns expressed by family and friends, and watching other men struggle. The fears can worm themselves into men's thinking and influence their behaviour without conscious awareness of their effects.[6] I hope reading this book will provide men with added insight into their actions and more understanding of their emotions, and loosen the binds of some of their preconceptions. Maybe they'll even be able to cut themselves a bit of slack, for one of the things I found is that men can be hard on themselves. When it comes to those of us who are partners of retiring men, I hope increasing our appreciation for what they are going through will make us more compassionate and help us hang on to our sense of humour.

When I told men I was writing this book, more often than not they would say, "It's not going to be depressing, is it?" I'm warning them that the next chapter is a bit of a downer because it looks at men's fears about retirement. But after that, the book turns to the reality of retirement, which puts most of those fears to bed. I'm confident my fretful friends will find the book thought-provoking, eye-opening and surprising. And I'm even guaranteeing them a few laughs. But depressing it isn't—because the story of men's retirement is primarily one of adjustment, revitalization and even reinvention.

Fears of Retirement

———•◦•———

When I asked men to describe the fears they had about retirement, many of them spoke in terms of loss. They worried that retirement would be a piling up of losses: loss of identity, loss of meaning to their lives, loss of intellectual stimulation, loss of structure to their day, loss of income. Some of their fears were based on watching other men handle retirement; other fears came from cultural images embedded in books they'd read, plays they'd attended, or TV shows or movies they'd watched. Some of the impressions had endured from adolescence and others were more recently acquired. It is a credit to the men I interviewed that they were able to recognize the impact of these deeply rooted ideas and willing to share their insights with others.

The first part of this chapter looks at those cultural influences. The second part explores men's attachment to work. Men's fears of retirement are exacerbated because, for the most part, they like what they do. Although most of the men I interviewed were frustrated with particular aspects of their job, and in some cases these frustrations were pushing them out the door, all of them could enumerate what they gained from working. And that's the second part of this chapter—an examination of what men lose when work ends and what they'll need to replace in retirement. As you'll read, the world of work looms large for the men of my generation, so it's not surprising they have fears about retirement.

Cultural Messages

We are told that retirement is one of the most complicated transitions men of my generation will experience in their lives. This makes sense when you realize that work has been central to their self-image and their masculinity. As boys, they were surrounded by cultural images of men as breadwinners and undisputed heads of the family. The role was epitomized in the popular TV series *Father Knows Best* about an idealized '50s nuclear family. There was the dad, Jim Anderson, who worked as manager of the General Insurance Company; Margaret, the stay-at-home mom; and the three children, Betty, Bud and Kathy. I don't remember ever seeing Jim at work, but at home he had it all—love, respect, power—and he didn't have to do any housework, iron any shirts or prepare any meals. The rite of passage that would gain a young man access to this world of men was getting his first paycheque. And having a job made you hot. Talcott Parsons, one of the most influential sociologists of the 1950s and '60s, summed up the cultural rule of the time: "A mature woman can love, sexually, only a man who takes his full place in the masculine world, above all its occupational aspect, and who takes responsibility for a family."[1]

We may think things changed when boomers got high and dropped out in the '60s, or when feminism liberated them to redefine gender roles. But the link between masculine self-identity and economic productivity has been very sticky. Gail Sheehy found this persistence when she interviewed men for her book *Understanding Men's Passages: Discovering the New Map of Men's Lives*. "Deep down, the way men see their role has remained surprisingly consistent. . . . Being a good provider is still the primary way men define themselves," she writes. "What has changed so drastically is that fewer men, and more and more women, can fulfill that role."[2]

To better understand the power of this cultural conditioning, I asked the men I interviewed to tell me about images that grip their imagination when they consider retiring from the world of work. Several of them singled out Arthur Miller's play *Death of a Salesman*, the tragedy of a man thrown in the dustbin at the end of his working life. Even though these men last read or saw the play performed many decades ago, the story still resonates with them. *Death of a Salesman* is the tale of Willy Loman, a salesman in his 60s with a wife and two grown sons. As the play opens, he has just returned home from a weekly sales trip through his New England territory. He is exhausted and has lost his mojo. He tells his wife, "I'm tired to the death. I couldn't make it. I just couldn't make it." The rest of the play is a downhill spiral and closes with Willy killing himself in the mistaken belief that the insurance money will leave his son with a nest egg.

The play is about the hollowness of the American dream, the lies we tell ourselves and others, and the fraught relationships between fathers and sons. It can also be read as a frightening tale of reaching the end of one's career. Willy feels that the nature of his business has changed, and he looks back longingly at the good old days. "In those days there was personality in it," he says. "There was respect, and comradeship, and gratitude in it. Today, it's all cut and dried, and there's no chance for bringing friendship to bear—or personality. You see what I mean? They don't know me any more."

Willy's wife argues that his boss should give him some concessions in light of his age. "But you're sixty years old," she says. "They can't expect you to keep traveling every week." When Willy meets with his boss to try to work something out, Willy reminds him that he has been on the road selling for the company since he was a teenager. "I was with the firm when your father used to carry you in here in his arms," he says. Willy admits he doesn't have the energy he used to and has come to the decision that he'd rather not travel any more. "Speaking frankly and between the two of us, y'know—I'm just a little tired," he says. The upshot of the meeting is that Willy is fired. The boss says there is no longer a spot for him with the company. "It's a business, kid, and everybody's gotta pull his own weight." Willy replies, "You can't eat the orange and throw the peel away—a man is not a piece of fruit!"[3]

When *Death of a Salesman* was performed in 1949, it was a sensation, winning six Tony Awards, and Miller received the 1949 Pulitzer Prize for Drama. Firsthand accounts report that after the first public performance of the play there was no applause. The audience was momentarily stunned into silence, followed by a tidal wave of crying and sobbing. Six decades later the story hasn't lost its power. After *New York Times* theatre critic Charles Isherwood reviewed a 2012 production of the play, he was inundated with responses from readers. He was struck by how eloquent, incisive and deeply felt the comments were and he quotes a man saying that the play haunted his father to his death "and it still continues to haunt me." Isherwood concluded that the drama speaks as powerfully to readers and viewers today as it did to audiences in 1949.[4]

On the surface, the story is a terrifying tale of the discarded older employee who was forcibly retired—a story guaranteed to heighten a man's anxiety about being prematurely yanked from the workforce. But a closer look reveals a much more nuanced relationship between Willy and the world of work. Willy actually had another job offer. When he faces unemployment, his next-door neighbour, Charley, offers him a position with decent pay and no requirement to go on the road. But Willy can't bring himself to accept the hand up. He is unable to swallow his pride and take a job from someone with whom he has always had a competitive relationship. Willy's downfall is his hubris, not his lack of employment opportunities.

Ben was one of the men I interviewed who talked about *Death of a Salesman* and its effect on his vision of retirement. "The role of Willy Loman had a real impact on me," he confessed. "In the play's final scene, I still remember what Loman's neighbour Charley said about Loman's life as a salesman. 'He's a man way out there in the blue, riding on a smile and a shoeshine.' Loman was a guy who had no intellectual basis in his life. The play was really about what was hollow in the American dream." At this point, Ben added emphatically, "I never identified with Willy Loman. I was Charley, not Willy Loman."

While Loman's tale plays out as a powerful tragedy, men are more likely to fear their own career will end with a whimper rather than a bang. And for some men that more banal conclusion is personified by the film character Warren Schmidt. Warren is a retiree played masterfully by Jack Nicholson in the 2002 movie *About Schmidt*. The film opens with a shot of Warren in his empty office in the Woodmen Insurance Company watching the clock tick down to 5 p.m. This is his last day of work and his files are stacked in boxes. Warren is an assistant vice-president, he is 66 years old and he is retiring after spending his working life at Woodmen. Warren's contribution is recognized with a retirement dinner at which his replacement encourages him to drop by the office any time he wants. "In fact," the new boss adds, "I might have some questions about our various products, like the new universal life policy we're launching next month."

The first day of Warren's retirement he wakes up at 7 a.m., puts on his dressing gown and sits at his desk doing a word scramble puzzle. When he takes the new boss up on his suggestion and drops into the office to offer his assistance, he is quickly shown the door. "You did a super job of handing things over," says the boss. "Just super. Smooth sailing all the way. If anything bubbles to the surface I'll be sure to give you a holler." As Warren leaves the building, he notices his file boxes, including boxes labelled "Active Files," piled up by the Dumpster.

The film shows a man thrown adrift from the anchor of work, and we watch as he tries to find some solid footing.

The sudden death of his wife shortly after he retires casts him further to sea. As the movie plays out, we accompany Schmidt on his many voyages of personal discovery. He travels to his daughter's wedding and, after unsuccessfully trying to get her to call off the ceremony, accepts that her life is hers to lead. He takes a trip down memory lane to visit childhood places and finds time has obliterated his presence. He becomes resigned to the fact that his career didn't live up to his boyhood dreams. "When I was a kid I used to think that maybe I was special," he says. "Somehow destiny had tapped me to be a great man. I got a degree in business and statistics and was planning to start my own business and build it up into a great corporation. I was going to be one of those guys you read about. But somehow it just didn't work out that way. You've got to remember I had a top-notch job at Woodmen and a family to support, and I couldn't exactly put their security at risk."

When I interviewed Leonard, he told me watching *About Schmidt* made him ponder his own retirement. He remembered thinking that the way Schmidt retired epitomized the opposite of his own retirement vision. "Because his career was such a downer," Leonard said, "Schmidt was trying to achieve in retirement the things that had eluded him so far. He bought the big RV and wanted to make a clear break from the rest of his life. I see my life after retirement as an extension of what I've been doing rather than being an abrupt change. It's a transition rather than a rupture."

When I interviewed Caulfield, he told me *About Schmidt* had a big impact on him—but not at first viewing. "When I first saw the film, it didn't mean much to me," he said. "But that was before I retired. Two years later I was retired and I could really relate. Schmidt is lost, unhinged, searching, finding and not finding, and drifting into obscurity. It is a great thought piece. It is not comforting and that's what gives it its power."

Once retired Schmidt has few ties to his pre-retirement life, especially after his wife dies. So when he is set adrift, it is as though he has never seen water before. It's understandable that Schmidt would be "lost, unhinged, searching," as Caulfield described. For the film's director, Alexander Payne, the movie is a statement about the conformity of current times, "a conformity that, among its many invisible effects, helps produce empty lost lives like Schmidt."[5] The movie is make-believe, and the reality of most people's retirement wouldn't make a tragic tale that could be turned into a box-office success. Leonard's description of retirement, as a continuum of one's life rather than an abrupt change, is the way most men retire. So they are able to draw on the passions, capacities and relationships that have characterized their pre-retirement lives. For them, retirement is not a cliff on life's road, it's another marker on the journey.

What Is Lost When Work Ends?

When work ends what exactly are men losing? I asked men what they got from their work, and they described an attachment that is profound and multi-faceted. They all enjoyed some aspect of their jobs, and for some "work is more fun than fun," as Noel Coward says. There's the collegiality of the workplace, the intellectual challenge, the adrenalin rush of deadlines, the satisfaction of a job well done, the structure work gives to your life, as well as the sense of purpose. You gain a certain status from work—among your peers, with your family and with yourself. And work gives you an income.

Here's Murray's description of what he gave up when he left his job. "I had built a super team," he said. "We were doing amazing stuff and had gotten into a position of national leadership on our work. So there was the plea-sure of success. Then there was the intellectual stimulation, getting to work with good people all across the country, and we had wonderful people to work with both inside and outside the company. Also, I'll admit—I am somewhat defined by what I do."

Duncan is the superintendent of a 55-unit apartment complex, a job he's been doing for over thirty years. "This job is good for my body and my brain," he told me. "I have to shovel the snow, mow the lawn and do repairs in the buildings. And I have to deal with all the tenant issues and interview new tenants." Duncan is too humble to admit that he's the linchpin in the whole operation but acknowledged that he's basically a one-man band and things don't function without him. "I try to not get sick because things fall apart very quickly," he said. "Although it's a bit of a burden to know management and the tenants are counting on me, it's also pretty satisfying." There's a side benefit to Duncan's job that he particularly appreciates. "Some of the tenants are new to the city or just arrived in Canada, and they don't have very much. I work with my church and other people to get them donations of clothing and furniture. I know it means a lot to them, especially when they have children."

Regardless of occupation, the satisfactions described by Murray and Duncan were experienced by all the men I interviewed—the fun of working with other people, solving problems and pushing yourself to get a job done, and done well. Also, the men often see their work as making a contribution—to someone, to something or to the greater good. That's a lot of benefits. It's no wonder that people fear the loss of these rewards and need to find replacements and make adjustments when work ends. One man said that losing his work was like losing a lover.

Some of the men I interviewed talked about confronting their losses as part of a mourning process that helped them say goodbye. Several said their adjustment to retirement followed the stages of grief and loss proposed by Elisabeth Kübler-Ross in her groundbreaking book *On Death and Dying* (denial and isolation, anger, bargaining, depression and acceptance).

It has become a truism to say that men gain their identity from work, and removing work rips that away. Victor talked about experiencing this loss of identity when his job ended, and I asked him to explain what the loss felt like. He replied, "Retirement means banishment and obscurity." The following quotation from William James's *The Principles of Psychology* (1890) seems to capture Victor's feeling of banishment and obscurity: "No more fiendish punishment could be devised, were such a thing physically possible, than that one should be turned loose in society and remain absolutely unnoticed by all the members thereof. If no one turned around when we entered, answered when we spoke, or minded what we did, but if every person we met 'cut us dead,' and acted as if we were non-existent things, a kind of rage and impotent despair would before long well up in us, from which the cruellest bodily torture would be a relief."[6] Victor told me he had struggled with coming to terms with his retirement and concluded, "I'm now at the acceptance stage of Kübler-Ross."

As well as giving one an identity, the workplace brings a routine and a structure to the day, which provides great psychological comfort. When I interviewed Ralph, he said one of people's great fears of retirement is losing the framework of working and not knowing what will replace it. "It's anxiety-making," Ralph said, "to contemplate moving from having every minute of the day defined for you to an open-ended day. This is a huge transition. When you work long hours and define yourself by your work, you might have nothing else in your life to fill the day—beyond your family, and maybe a cottage—but that's not enough."

The way the trappings of the workplace offer sustenance and support is graphically conveyed in Franz Kafka's chilling 1925 novel *The Trial*. The bank employee, Joseph K., has been arrested on charges for which he can get no information. The unexpected arrest takes place when he is at home, getting out of bed in the morning and still in his nightshirt. He feels this random and intrusive event never could have happened at work, because the routine and structure of his workplace would have protected him. "In the Bank, for instance, I am always prepared," says Joseph K., "nothing of that kind could possibly happen to me there, I have my own attendant, the general telephone and the office telephone stand before me on my desk, people keep coming in to see me, clients and clerks, and above all, my mind is always on my work and so kept on the alert, it would be an actual pleasure to me if a situation like that cropped up in the Bank."[7]

When I interviewed Ernest, he described the process of leaving the structure of his work as going from the known to the unknown. "I had my family obligations," he said. "And I belong to an outdoors club where I've been spending a day a week for the past twenty-five years working on a project. But that still left a lot of free time. And I need to be busy—after only a week at the cottage I'm ready to move on. So I knew I had to find some way to contribute something of social value. I needed to find my passion. But when I first retired I had no idea what that would be, and that was a worry. My anxiety was fuelled when I got this advice from a retired neighbour. 'The secret is not to book your haircut and your visit to the bank manager in the same week.' I was appalled and thought, 'This guy is on the downward slide.'"

Like many men I interviewed, Ernest feared that once the structure of work was removed he'd be left with a vacuum. And then, like his neighbour, he'd end up stretching out appointments to fill the void. Other men feared they'd fill the void with more worrisome pastimes. When I interviewed Ben, he said flat out, "I'm afraid of retirement. I'm afraid of not having enough to do and having to watch that I don't drink too much. For this reason, I'm probably working longer than I need to."

Some men said this empty form of retirement was epitomized in John Updike's Pulitzer Prize–winning novel *Rabbit at Rest*. Harry "Rabbit" Angstrom has retired to Florida in the winter and mourns his glory days as his high school's basketball star. The book closes with his death from a heart attack, which was brought about when he showed off his athletic prowess to a teenager shooting hoops on a neighbourhood court. Updike's picture of Rabbit as a six-foot-three ex-athlete "weighing two-thirty at the least" is powerfully drawn, as is Rabbit's life in retirement. Florida, with its low pale buildings that "cater especially to illness and age," drains the spirit out of him. "Friendship has a thin, provisional quality, since people might at any minute buy another condominium and move to it, or else up and die." The big question Rabbit wants to ask his golf buddies, but doesn't, is: "Help me, guys. Tell me how you've got on top of sex and death so they don't bother you."[8] Updike allows Rabbit a modest redemption through a deathbed reconciliation with his estranged wife and son, but it's a gloomy tale.

When I interviewed Ben, he said the image of retirement Updike paints in *Rabbit at Rest* has stayed with him since he read the book some decades ago. "The book pretty much describes the emptiness that could happen to me or anybody," he admitted. "But Rabbit ends up in Florida all alone. The difference for me is that I have both a family and a community, and I'm not planning on changing that."

When I spoke to Hal, he said he was so anxious to avoid the retirement that Updike portrays that he has reduced the amount of time he and his wife spend in Florida. When he initially retired, they went for three months straight and now they only go one week per month during the winter. "When we were first down in Florida my son came to visit us," he recalled. "He said to me, 'When I see you sitting by the pool you look old.' His comment really got to me. I started thinking about a quote from the actress Katharine Hepburn who said we have an obligation to be interesting. Down there I don't think anybody has ever asked me a personal question. So many people when they leave work become frozen in time and they are the same person— months later, years later—as they were on the last day of work. There is no personal growth."

This fear of stagnating from loss of intellectual stimulation was a frequent theme when I interviewed men about retiring. There is an assumption that being in the world of work forces you to stay in the game mentally and provides you with a level of intellectual stimulation that's harder to find when you're retired. Although many men found this not to be the case once they retired, the fear is deep-rooted. It is often exacerbated by watching friends or family who have let themselves slide.

Willis's wife told me that Willis needs intellectual stimulation and his anxieties about retirement were aggravated by watching her father retire. "My father was retired for thirty-four years, and his life became a dull social pattern with too much of the same kind of people," she said. "He and my mother were not challenged enough, and retirement slowed them down. It really bothered Willis that part of Dad's daily ritual was to have a drink at noon." Willis agreed that he is afraid of having his father-in-law's life. "I worry retirement will mean isolation and loss of intellectual challenge," he said. "I fear losing the sense of meaning for my life."

Stewart doesn't want to follow in his father-in-law's footsteps either. "He's been retired for thirty years and, at first, he was pretty happy doing nothing," he said. "But it caught up to him." His wife described why her father is an anti-role model for Stewart. "My dad is a perfect example of why you need to have something meaningful in your life through your older years," she said. "When Dad stopped work at age 63 or 64, it was a total stop. Some people have interests they have deferred when they're working due to a lack of energy or time. Retirement lets them go back to school or do projects or research they've been putting off. My father didn't have those interests. His focus was work and family, so retirement left him with a lot of free time. He had been a superb athlete as a young man, and over time, faced with his failing physical abilities, he began to drink heavily. He figured there were no expectations, so there was no reason to monitor his drinking."

For Ernest it was his own father who provided the model of how not to retire. "My father didn't retire until he was in his 80s and then he retired terribly," Ernest said. "He died two years later, and he was a miserable guy for those years. He made my mother's life very difficult as he tried to manage her. I remember him being furious that Mom had left the skins on the tomatoes in the salad that she had prepared for him for lunch. He couldn't bear not having a life purpose. My takeaway lesson is 'Make sure you have some interesting stuff to do when you retire.' And when it comes to your spouse, the rule is 'For better or worse but not for lunch.' You need some other interests."

As well as observing the way the older generation retired, the men I interviewed were watching one another. Patrick told me that conversations with his retired colleagues could be pretty short, and he was worried he would end up in the same boat. "After you get through the golf, repairing things at the cottage and fixing the pool down south," he said, "you pretty quickly don't have many other things to talk about." Patrick went on to describe a conversation he recently had on this topic. "I was just speaking to someone about a mutual friend who checked out in his early 60s. He has a lovely cottage and a place in Florida. It sounds like a pretty nice lifestyle. But when I asked my friend how our mutual friend was doing, he answered, 'I don't make much of an effort to contact him anymore. We have nothing to talk about.'"

Along with losing the structure and stimulation of the workplace comes the loss of employment income. Having to rely on pensions or retirement savings is a worry for some men. As Barry put it: "People get addicted to cash flow. You can't turn off the tap first. First you have to adapt the lifestyle. You need to plan ahead, make the lifestyle changes, and then you are ready to turn off the tap. But the hard part is making those changes."

For David's part he's not worried about the financial implications of his own retirement: it's his wife's retirement that concerns him. "Right now her work is very time-consuming," he told me, "but when she's not working she's in the stores. I'm worried about those bills when she becomes a full-time shopper." David might appreciate this joke that another interviewee told me. One man says to his friend, "It is so sweet. I saw you walking along the street holding your wife's hand." The response: "If I let go, she shops."

Many of the fears men have about retirement are embedded in our use of the word *retire*. When we tell people we are going to *retire* for the night, we mean we're going to sleep or calling it a day. To *retire* from a particular place is to take oneself off or shut oneself away. So the very idea of retirement embodies all the fears the men expressed:

banishment, isolation, emptiness, lack of stimulation. Fears are valuable when they alert us to imminent danger because they can push us to take evasive action. But inaccurate stereotypes can inhibit action or direct people down dead ends. The next chapter separates the realistic fears from the false assumptions, so men won't waste time worrying about the wrong things.

The Reality of Retirement

Are men's fears about retirement realized, and do our cultural stereotypes hold true? This section looks at the reality of men's retirement, including whether they can expect the arrival of those dreaded Ds of drink, depression, divorce and death. The first reality check concerns the very definition of retirement. The fictional characters of Willy Loman, Warren Schmidt and Rabbit Angstrom all have a binary relationship with work—either on or off, working or not working. But this doesn't reflect the reality of retirement for many men. Retirement often comprises a much more ambiguous and fluid relationship with the world of work. In fact it appears to be as much a state of mind as an economic condition.

The statisticians tell us that in 2014 about four out of five Canadian males aged 65 or over were not in the workforce.[1] Before I started my research, I figured this was a straightforward way of calculating how many men were retired. As I learned from my interviews, I shouldn't have made any such assumption. Some of the men who are not currently in the workforce will have retired, but others may be actively looking for work. Others are retired for the time being but will decide at a later time to go back to work. And then there are those who are not in the workforce as defined by Statistics Canada, but who do not consider themselves to be retired. The following description of some of the men I interviewed will introduce you to the many faces of retirement.

Darryl eased out of income-earning activity and eased into becoming a self-defined retiree. He is 67 and used to run an international consulting business. When contracts started drying up, he wasn't quite ready to retire, but he now thinks his income-earning days are over. "Around age 62 I found it harder and harder to find new gigs," he said. "When you run your own business, retirement is somewhere between the time when you're not quite as interested in working and the time when nobody calls you anymore. It took me a year to get to the point where I would answer 'retired' when people asked me what was my occupation."

Ernest has been out of the paid workforce for decades but treats his volunteer responsibility like a full-time job. Statistics Canada may call him retired. However, that's not the way he sees it. He's 76 years old and left his job twenty years ago. Several months after leaving paid work, he accepted a demanding position in the non-profit world. He sometimes works as hard in his volunteer capacity as he did in his paid job. Although he stopped earning a wage decades ago, the word *retired* is not part of his self-definition.

Rupert is 74 and retired from his job at age 65. He doesn't consider himself retired because he continues to do research on subjects that were part of his career. "There are a number of definitions of retirement," he said. "In the eyes of others, I would be thought of as retired. But I do odd bits of contract work that interest me. Because I get to pick and choose, 'semi-retired' would be my self-definition. But I suppose, from a wage-earning perspective, I am retired. Whatever you call it, it's a privilege to work on my own projects and not be beholden to anyone."

At 72 years of age, Willis is well past retirement age but says he is not retired, he is unemployed. His last job ended sooner than he expected, and he is actively looking for another one. His goal is to land a position that comes with a five-year commitment. "I'm leading the working life I expect my son will have," he said, "because I've had six or seven different careers. When my last job ended, I wasn't ready. So I have to balance the books with another job. I would only stop working if I felt fed up or not able to give it my best shot."

Ralph is 63 and left his job after making a commitment to himself that he would retire when he turned 60. Then he got lured back by his employer. He would define himself as semi-retired and trying to fully retire. "I don't derive any particular benefit from my profession," he admitted. "I have a lot of other interests that I want to pursue before I get old and doddering. Work has always been a means to an end for me. When age 60 rolled around, because of the economic downturn of 2008/09, I wasn't where I wanted to be financially, but I was determined to stick to my retirement schedule." Not long after Ralph retired, his employer asked him to come back part-time and promised they'd make it work for him. "I don't have to report to anyone, and there is no hourly requirement," he said. "My wife and I can still spend five months a year on the road. I've been doing this for three years now, and I guess I'll do it for a while longer. I was totally prepared to go cold turkey on leaving work, and I believe I could have done it well, but this deal makes the transition to full retirement a lot easier."

I gained additional insight into men's varied relationships with retirement when I posed the question: When people ask you what you do, what is your answer? This is the moment at a cocktail party when someone is looking for a one-line response that sums up your status in the world of work. Here's how my interviewees responded.

Rupert told me this question always bothers him. "I say I'm retired," he said, "but then people ask 'What *did* you do?' It implies that now I don't do anything, and that the only interesting part of my life is what I used to do. But

I've never been busier, and I have all sorts of interesting commitments."

Some people have modified their responses over time. "I used to say I was in transition," Ryan said, "but I've evolved in my thinking. Now I say I'm retired, and I mention my former career, and that helps people situate me."

Several men said they referenced their former job or current interests in order to steer the conversation in that direction. Ernest tells people about the community development project he heads up, "because that's what I want to talk about." Leonard gives a quick summary of what he used to do and concludes with, "And now I'm fishing."

Gerry intends to retire from work in a few months but says he's not planning to tell people he's retired. "I'll say that I'm between jobs," he explained. "If they then ask what I do, I'll reply, 'Anything I want.'"

Many of the men I interviewed deflected the question with humour, as you can see from these responses.

Caulfield said, "I tell people I'm trying as hard as I can to do nothing, but it's very difficult, and I'm not always successful."

Terry alternates between these two responses: "I gave up my highly trained job so I could learn what it was to be an efficient houseboy," and "I've tried to do nothing so I'd learn what it was to be bored. But it hasn't worked out."

Victor tells people, "I'm working hard at being retired."

Colin says, "I'm a ski bum."

Willis had been responding to the question of what he does with the answer, "I think." But recently he decided to modify his reply and substitute the poet and philosopher Paul Valéry's variation on Descartes. "Sometimes I think, sometimes I am."

Adjustment to Retirement

After men retire, do they struggle to come to terms with their new state? The answer is yes in the short run. But, in the long run, most men adjust to retirement, and many men thrive. That's what the men I interviewed told me, and that's what the research shows. One survey found that only about 18 per cent of those who had been retired six months or less felt they were completely adjusted. The statistics rose to 35 per cent after two years in retirement, to 41 per cent with three to four years, and to 55 per cent after five or more years. After eleven or more years, four in five retirees felt completely adjusted.[2] But what a lot of research fails to capture is the bonus of retirement—the unanticipated pleasure many men derive from experiences that were only available to them because they weren't working.

What helps men make an adjustment to retirement is having multiple or possible selves. Psychologists Paul Baltes and Peter Graf call this our "system of selves"; if one self is challenged (let's say an athlete has an injury), then another self (maybe being a lover of music) is there to take its place. A critical aspect of this resiliency is the ability to change one's goals or aspirations in the face of reality. The good news is that we get better at this as we age. As Baltes and Graf found, "Older adults seem to become more flexible in accommodating their life goals to new circumstances, rather than being goal-tenacious."[3] This flexibility helps us maintain our self-esteem and sense of personal control as we age and change.

When I interviewed Hal, he described how his system of selves helped him adjust to retirement. "I always thought it was important to have a number of lily pads," he said, "and if one goes soft you can stand on another. If you allow work to define you completely, you are in deep trouble. When I was working, people relied on me, but the day I left, I was remembered for ten minutes. It's like taking a bucket out of the ocean: the hole is filled in almost immediately." After retiring, Hal struggled for a few months to find his footing, but now, eight years later, he's "pulling it off with great success and pleasure." "My first day of retirement I walked all day," he said. "I had no notion of who I was or what I would do. I had to find reasons to get out of the house and replace the psychic income I had enjoyed at my workplace. So I joined a gym because I had to have some structure, and then I found some volunteer opportunities. Now I have a full dance card, with most of it around my university contacts. And I'm learning French and practising piano. My goal is to keep growing personally and socially. I have so many things I want to do."

With this vivid description, Hal gives us insight into his process of adjustment and how he went about filling the void that was left when work ended. A critical piece of forging his new path was acknowledging that his work environment was going to move on without him—and quickly. Several of my interviewees found it tough to accept the loss of this workplace connection and their former identity. When I interviewed Wallace, he said he was taken aback by the finality of the rupture and the speed with which it all happened. "It was a shock," he said, "to go from being someone very much in the know about so many things and very connected, to realize how quickly that political capital fails. Also, I was surprised at how quickly old employers stop dealing with you once you're gone. There's no acknowledgement that you still exist. There is a complete lack of courtesy. So you narrow down quickly to home and family. You really need to get a feeling of self-worth from something other than who you used to be."

Wallace responded by creating a life post-work that includes volunteering with several non-profit organizations, reading, spending months travelling to visit widespread family, and hitting the gym several times a week. "My wife and I had a vision of retirement where we would do things that were mutually satisfying," he said, "and we've largely succeeded in doing that." When I interviewed Wallace's wife, she felt that his retirement had been "a piece of cake" because he always had other interests. "While others seem to be terrified about retirement," she said, "this was never an issue for Wallace. On our first date many decades ago, Wallace asked me where I wanted to live when I retired. I was a bit taken aback. I was in my early 30s at the time, and I had never thought about it. But Wallace always thought he would retire at 60, and he talked for decades about the *troisième âge* that began after your work life. He always had things he wanted to participate in that he didn't have time for while he was working."

Rupert was another of my interviewees who found his lifelong interests eased his departure from the workplace. "My projects were totally transportable to retirement," he said. "I began transcribing one particular journal twenty-six years ago, and I remember thinking at the time this was something I might want to work on later. Well, that time has come. I have a colleague visiting me now, and we're working on some research together. I've found it's good to team up with someone to keep myself motivated. Also, I'm a fact checker for a book. I'm preparing a paper for a conference, and I still get requests to give speeches about a book I published some years ago. I've never been busier. These commitments keep me going."

However, some men don't have lifelong interests, especially interests of the consuming nature that Rupert described. For them, the early stage of retirement can be a process of exploration as they try things on for size. This is a natural part of a life transition. In his book *Transitions: Making Sense of Life's Changes*, the late William Bridges describes transitions as having three phases: endings, neutral zones and new beginnings. He says the neutral zone is a process of disorientation and reorientation, and the natural reaction can be to rush in to fill the void with activity. Bridges says this happens because "we are not used to taking time out to be by ourselves and to reflect on what has gone by and what is coming next."[4]

Caulfield took the time to reflect and to stay in the void that Bridges describes before moving on to a new beginning. When I interviewed him, he described what it was like to go through the transition to retirement. "At the end, my workplace situation was very toxic," he said, "so, in some ways, leaving made me feel healthier. It made it easier to wipe my hands of work. But I had loved my career and found it fulfilling in many different ways, so there was sadness and regret and longing. It was like leaving a lover. I realized it was better not to jump right into another work relationship. I needed to find myself. So I started looking back at my life, and this work has brought me some moments of beauty, some of regret, some of sadness. It's been a search for meaning and a time to explore. It's been a fascinating voyage. I'm doing a weird hodgepodge of things including biking, gardening and travel. Sometimes I feel guilty for being egocentric and allowing myself this luxury of time. It seems very self-indulgent. But I believe the good you do for others, you can do in small ways. Everything has become so personal to me, and the interior is now the exterior. The last time I remember doing this was when I was 14 or 15 and then when I was 23. It's difficult but also empowering to have the luxury of looking back over one's life. So I am taking this time, although it hasn't been easy."

While Caulfield has given himself permission to spend time in Bridges' "neutral zone," some men find it hard to carve out space for themselves in the face of competing demands. This has been Albert's experience. "It's been eighteen months since I retired," he said, "and I am still trying to slow down to the speed of life. My big issue is keeping control over my time. Too many people and organizations ask for your help to achieve their goals, and their goals may not align with your plans. What I would like is more 'me days' for walking, gardening, creating, visiting and thinking." When Albert was working, his relationship to work had been "total engagement," but then it stopped completely. "That chapter of my life closed," he said. "They're so busy at work, I don't even go over for a coffee." He refocused his energy on retirement. "Particularly towards the end of my career, I found that my schedule left little time and energy to visit with family and friends, pursue my hobbies and do my volunteer activities, including having the chance to help others," he said. "Now I'm busy around the house, volunteer six to ten hours per week at church, explore my region and province, and help friends with their projects and them with mine, quid pro quo. On rare occasions, I feel that I have touched a sense of peace, but it is only a touch, not a landing."

When I interviewed Albert's wife, she said he has latched onto his retirement responsibilities and attacked them as though he were still working. "Albert is approaching retirement with absolute intensity," she said. "His drive is still alive and kicking, and I wish he'd settle down a bit and chill out. But it's easy to understand why he has problems saying no to people. He's a very giving person and the best team player I've ever known. He always has his radar up for other people's needs. He brings all the old ladies who can't drive over here for dinner Christmas Eve, and then we drive them to the church service. Things like this fill his life. If he ever winds up in a nursing home, he'll be the one opening the door for everyone else."

One of the many things that will serve Albert well in retirement is his capacity for friendship. The research is mounting that having friends means we'll be healthier and happier, and men told me their friendships are making it

easier to adjust to retirement. Some research has distin-
guished between work friends and non-work friends and
found that well-adjusted retirees were more likely to have
non-work friends in their social circle.[5]

When British writer Somerset Maugham visited the
United States, he noted that the men he met had a host of
acquaintances, but few had friends. "They have business
associates, playmates at the bridge table or on the golf links,
buddies they fish or shoot or sail with, boon companions
they drink with, comrades they fight with, but that is all."
He only knew two men whom he considered to be close
friends. "They will arrange to dine together and spend the
evening in desultory conversation because they enjoy one
another's society. They have no secrets from one another,
and each is interested in the other's concerns because they
are his." He found the scarcity of deep friendships surprising because Americans are sociable, amicable and cordial.
"The only explanation I can offer myself is that the pace
of life in the United States is so great that few men have
time for friendship. Leisure is needed for acquaintance to
deepen into intimacy. Another possible explanation is that
in America when a man marries his wife engulfs him."[6]

Maugham's observations support the truism that men
have few friends beyond their workplace colleagues and,
if married, are dependent on their spouses for companion-
ship. While many of the men I interviewed would have

liked more time during their working life to hang out with friends, most have the kind of golfing, fishing and sailing buddies that Maugham dismisses, and some of them are close friends. Retirement allows men to make up for lost time, and they're reconnecting with pals from their past, solidifying existing friendships or cultivating new ones. They're meeting friends for lunches, organizing get-togethers at coffee shops, and running book clubs. Let's take Albert as an example. Some of his friends are lifelong, but he's also forming a new network of fellow retirees. "I've been pursuing one of my hobbies for fifty years," he said, "and I meet regularly with long-standing friends who share that passion. But I'm finding the number of newly retired men I know is ramping up. We are sharing our initial retirement adventures at weekly coffee meetings and other events."

What speaks well to men's capacity for building and sustaining relationships in retirement is that some of the men who are making the most of their friendships relocated when they left work. Although they're living in a new location and are physically removed from their former connections, they're finding ways to maintain old friendships and develop new ones. This has been the case for Terry, who moved to another province immediately upon leaving his job. When I interviewed his wife, she talked about the important role his new friends were playing in supporting his retirement. "All his very good friends are retired," she said, "and these are very strong friendships for him. They go out for coffee and once a week they get together to play pool. They are all good readers, and they have interesting conversations. They discuss the books they've read and the issues of the day. These relationships are very important to Terry because the men are still 'with it'—they're engaged in the world."

In Darryl's new retirement location, he has become the "socio-emotional leader" of his group of male friends. "I'm the guy who organizes birthday parties and lunches and meetings at the bar," he said. "I get great satisfaction out of that. And to do it right you have to put yourself in the position of the other people. What I see is how much people enjoy that, and it is from their happiness I'm beginning to get mine. So in the future I've decided I'm going to do things that make other people happy. If there is anything I would fault myself for in life, it is being too self-absorbed. But I find I'm moving away from that and becoming more empathetic."

Retirement provides the luxury of time that allows men to head off on extended trips with friends and have the kinds of adventures that create strong bonds. When I interviewed Gerry, he told me that having the opportunity to travel with his friends was one of the great advantages of retirement. "My buddies have gone on a cycling trip every year for twenty years," he said, "and because of my work commitments I've never been able to join them. Now I can." Leonard told me that because he no longer had the pressing demands of full-time work, he recently spent several weeks hanging out with two college friends, fishing, hiking and exploring. "We live in three different countries now, and the only reason we were able to coordinate our schedules and make this trip happen is because all three of us are retired or semi-retired."

When we looked earlier at men's fears of retirement, one of their worries was losing their intellectual edge and becoming less interesting to themselves and to others. The men I interviewed are making certain this doesn't happen by taking courses, participating in discussion groups and pursuing their own courses of study. They're also having those stimulating conversations with friends that Terry's wife described. When I asked Terry how he's spending his time now that he's retired, he gave me a sheepish grin and told me that he's working on figuring out the meaning of life. "I am struggling with the philosophical implications of mortality," he said. "So being retired means I can go down to my office and read and work away. The joy of being on my own schedule is that I'm reading a lot more, and not just mysteries. I've spent my life as a reader but didn't do much during my later working years, and now I'm catching up."

Some men I interviewed are using travel as a focus for their intellectual pursuits. Ralph and his wife spend about five months a year on the road, often staying one month at a time in a given location. "The focus is always different," Ralph said. "I am interested in art, architecture, design, food, literature and music. I design a trip around each city and do a lot of reading for every one. As well as being intellectually stimulating, our trips are very social. We get visits from friends who happen to be passing through, and meet new people."

Some men who have been working at desk jobs their whole lives see retirement as a chance to use their hands and their backs. Colin maintains several properties that are owned by his extended family, and they require constant attention. He finds this commitment, combined with caring for his two dogs, is enough to keep him occupied. "My dream for retirement was to work with a backhoe," he says. "You don't have to think all the time. For the past twenty-five years, my brother-in-law and I have been looking after a family property that was built around 1860. I have taken it apart and put it back together, and maintaining it is a part-time job. We spend all summer there. Worrying about how I would fill my day has not been an issue. I had no anxieties about retirement. While I enjoyed working at the time, I don't miss it." Clayton is another retiree who has been happy to have the chance to do some physical labour. He had a desk job but learned construction trades while working with his father when he was young. He has loved being part of the construction crew on his cottage. "I'm happy as a clam digging, hammering and drilling in the floor."

Doing more volunteer work is a priority for many men once they retire. Some men, while they were working, found time to serve on volunteer boards, get involved in fundraising or work on the frontline. Others feel they have neglected community work and are keen to make amends in retirement. After Ernest retired, he found a volunteer job that he describes as being the perfect fit. "I really need a sense of public purpose," he said. "It's the do-gooder in me. I spend thirty to forty hours a week working with my organization, and it's the perfect retirement gig because it combines all my skills and interests." Ernest thinks retirement can be wonderful as long as you have a passion for something—"a fire in your belly." He recognizes that not everyone could do a lot of volunteering while they were in the workforce, but he says it's never too late to give back. "With a little coaching and networking you can get into this wonderful activity," he told me.

Gerry sees the opportunity to volunteer as one of the big draws of retirement. "I want to work in our local soup kitchen," he said. "And there's an international organization that my wife and I have been involved with for ten years. They have asked us to go on one of their trips, and now I can. My mother has always done extensive volunteer work, including lots of work with her church. That's the same with the rest of my family. I've been the corporate guy who booked out and I'd like to change that."

Some men put their workplace experience to good use in mentoring the next generation. Harold shares "war stories" with business students on weekend retreats and provides guidance to women's organizations. "I'm the mentor to a group of women that have made me an honorary female," he said.

After Murray retired, he started volunteering with a local organization and appreciates the way it's helped him get to know his city better. "Up to now I've had very little concern about the local level of government, and this organization is very city-dependent. I've been working with them for seven to eight years and am currently on the board. There are times when I'm putting in forty hours per week. But the big difference between volunteering and work is that you can go away for three months on a trip without any difficulties, as long as you set it up in advance."

Gene Cohen, the late professor of psychiatry, spent decades studying people over sixty and helping them get more out of their later years. In his book *The Mature Mind: The Positive Power of the Aging Brain*, Cohen reports that the people who were the most satisfied with their retirement were those who had found meaningful volunteer experiences and other ways to give back.[7] Doing good made them happy. Cohen's findings are echoed in the results of the well-known Harvard Study of Adult Development conducted by Dr. George Vaillant. The research found that people who gave of themselves for community building and guiding the next generation tripled their chances that their 70s would be a time of joy rather than despair. Vaillant calls this stage in adult development *generativity*.[8]

Regardless of what people choose to do in retirement, research finds they'll adjust better if their activities have higher personal value and are ones in which they're more emotionally invested. Retirees who feel retirement is for resting and relaxing are less satisfied with their lives and their retirement. "Psychologically, they feel less socially connected, less productive and valued, less confident, less optimistic about the future—and much less motivated—compared to those who consider retirement to be a time to pursue new goals."[9] Hal remembers being very dissatisfied with the first six to eight months of his retirement because he was only resting and relaxing. "I was watching too much TV and had no personal growth," he said. "Things weren't in focus." Albert is also wary of the rest and relaxation model of retirement and finds TV to be the "biggest time waster of all time." He's also conscious of the time he's "spent and lost" on the Internet and social media. "Hours, days, weeks and months can quickly disappear if one gets addicted to social media," he warns. "It seems to me that things on the computer always take longer than expected."

Some of the benefits men told me they experienced in retirement were those they anticipated. They assumed they would have more time for friends and family, and more hours to work on their own projects and pursue personal interests. But retirement also offered up unexpected pleasures, both big and small.

Unexpected Pleasures of Retirement

When it comes to unexpected pleasures of retirement, family and friends feature prominently. For many men, not working has given them the time to provide support—both emotional and physical—to their nearest and dearest. Some men have been able to be with their elderly relatives at the end of their lives, and some are providing ongoing eldercare. Some have nursed spouses, other family members or friends through injury or illness. Some retired men are taking on more of the role of nurturer and counsellor with their adult children, a role that was formerly their partner's domain.

Men with grandchildren report on the joy they derive from hanging out with the youngest generation and the priority it has assumed in their lives. Rupert said that one of his retirement goals was to be closer to his family, and being freed from his office allows him the luxury of spending long stretches of time with children and grandchildren who are located across the country.

Murray's wife said retirement has transformed his relationships with family and friends. "When Murray's mom was dying of cancer he moved in with her," she said, "and he didn't come home until after she died. He was her primary caregiver for months, and he had no agenda other than to be with her. After that, my mom broke her leg, and then her hip, and she lived with us for three months. We had a caregiver in the mornings, and Murray looked after her in the afternoons. All this caring for the elderly was only possible because of Murray's retirement. As well, he's been to visit our grandson twice as often as I have. And he's generally taken over my social secretary role, which I really appreciate. When he was working, our friendships tended to be organized by me. After he retired, he began to solidify new friendships and has worked on rekindling old friendships."

Being semi-retired allowed Darryl to become the primary caregiver for his father-in-law during the last year of his life. Darryl and his father-in-law lived on separate continents, and Darryl travelled back and forth, spending every other month with him. "One of the things that has given me the greatest satisfaction in life was taking care of my wife's dad," he says. "I found out that I am actually good at that kind of thing. I'm good at finding solutions and reconciling competing needs, and that can be applied to caring for others. I don't think there was at a time ever before when somebody actually needed me."

Stewart was able to be part of the palliative care team for his dying mother, and, a few years later, for his dying aunt. In both cases he had to relocate himself to their cities and move into their homes. "A year after I left my job, my mother was diagnosed with pancreatic cancer," he says, "and I was able to spend the last two months of her life with her. Two years later my aunt fell ill and I spent the last six weeks of her life with her. These were the most awful and the most beautiful experiences of my life, and they would have been impossible if I'd been working full-time."

Here are more of retirement's unexpected pleasures cited by the men I interviewed:

- Not being bound by the expectations of others.
- The satisfaction that comes from being able to say no.
- Not having to suffer the fools you were job-bound to endure in the past.
- Being able to be blunt with people without having to consider whether they are a potential client or existing customer.
- Not having to go to those endless meetings.
- Being able to spend more time with people. Just dropping in or being able to say, "Let's go have a coffee."

- Not having to drive to work in traffic, particularly when it's snowing or icy.
- Not having to wear a suit and tie, a uniform or other form of work garb.
- Enjoying a nice long bath while listening to a radio documentary.
- Being able to take the side roads rather than the highway because you have the luxury of time.
- Being able to be more relaxed while doing things. Taking time to stop and get a drink, stretch one's legs or smell the proverbial roses.
- Having the time to talk and engage in those little personal encounters, like chatting with the cashier.
- Listening to the birds.
- Getting up at 7 a.m. rather than 5:30 a.m. Not having to set the alarm. Not being sleep deprived.

And then there are the domestic joys of cooking, gardening, home maintenance and even housework that are bringing some men more satisfaction than they ever imagined. These pleasures and the joys of deepening connections with your partner are talked about in *Relationships*.

The men I interviewed may have encountered some bumps adjusting to retirement, but they seem determined to live this stretch of their lives as consciously and fully as possible and to create a rich and satisfying future for themselves. The next two sections look at the facts about money and health, and examine some of the more flagrant stereotypes. They also show that the odds of living well in retirement are in favour of the retiring man.

Money

What about men's fear that they will not have enough money in retirement? Although most people will have less income once they retire, in most cases, it will be enough. Statistics Canada reports that the average Canadian in his late 70s has a family income level that corresponds to 80 per cent of what he had in his mid–50s.[10] However, family spending usually drops as well. Statistics Canada estimates that retired households spend about 67 per cent of what they spent prior to retirement. You're probably leaping to the same conclusion I did: people spend less because they have less to spend. But research shows that the majority of people reduce consumption in retirement by choice, rather than by constraint. This finding was contained in a 2015 report by McKinsey & Company that concluded people overestimate how much they will need to maintain the standard of living they had before retirement.[11]

Many people I interviewed said they were surprised to find they could live on less without hardship. Terry said that his retirement income is probably less than half of what it was when he was working. "But we still live comfortably, not extravagantly," he said. "We just live a little bit more carefully." His wife agreed. "I have a horrendous fear of being poor and have fretted about our finances, but it's all worked out well," she said. "It's costing us less than we thought to live. Our house is paid for, and we don't eat out that much, but we still do most of what we want. So it has been a surprise that we have had no financial issues. I think my worries have been unnecessary. You do have to plan for retirement, but you don't have to be as anxious about it as we thought."

A 2014 Ipsos Reid poll found that eight out of ten Canadians were confident they would be able to take care of basic living expenses in retirement. But when people were asked whether there was a serious risk they might outlive their retirement savings, there was a big difference between retirees and working people. Only 14 per cent of retirees were afraid of outliving their savings compared to 36 per cent of working people.[12] One of the big differences is that people on the cusp of retirement seem to be accumulating the most debt. Jonathan Chevreau reports in the *Financial Post* that a rising share of the heavily indebted is over 45 years of age, an age when people should be socking away savings ahead of retirement. Low interest rates have seduced boomers into taking on more debt to support their lifestyles, and these same low interest rates are eroding their retirement savings.[13]

Chevreau says his baby boomer contemporaries fall into two camps: the unemployed or the underemployed with no savings and growing debts, who could fall from the middle class into financial survival mode, especially in the event of divorce; and, at the other extreme, the fully employed, dual income couples who have been saving for the past three decades or have employer-sponsored defined-benefit pension plans. The 2015 report by McKinsey & Company looked more closely at those at risk of having a lower standard of living when they stopped working and estimated the number at 17 per cent of households. The "unprepared households" were middle- to high-income households that didn't contribute enough to retirement plans or group RRSPs, did not have access to an employer plan, or had below-average personal savings. The low-income households were in better shape because they often received as much income from government programs such as Old Age Security and Guaranteed Income Supplement as they had from working.[14]

For many of the men I interviewed, saving for retirement was a priority. In Rupert's case a lifetime of being fiscally conservative is paying off now. "We've never been great borrowers," he said. "We always pay off our credit cards, and our house is paid for. We have no extravagances. But we still manage to travel. And we've been able to set our kids up in their primary residences. I have no idea why people think they need so much to retire on." Rupert's wife agreed that finances had not been an issue in retirement. "We're careful," she said, "and we don't have grand needs. But we still manage to realize our dreams. We were able to use an inheritance to renovate our attic into a lovely workspace for me, and we bought ourselves a little place out East so we can spend more time visiting my daughter and her family."

When Murray took early retirement, he did the calculations to make sure he and his wife would be able to manage financially. For him the big issue was getting a grip on their expenditures, what he calls their "burn rate." "If you don't have massive monthly bills to pay," he said, "you have so much more control over your life. We don't have debt, and our children are no longer a financial draw. I knew we could have a reasonable lifestyle even if I retired." Murray's wife agreed that finances were not a worry when he retired. "We had been building our nest egg all along," she said. "It helps that our children are no longer on the payroll. And it helps, to use my grandmother's expression, that Murray is 'as tight as the bark of a young birch tree.'"

Rupert and Murray sound like case studies for *The Real Retirement*, a book by financial advisors Fred Vettese and Bill Morneau. The subtitle of their book is *Why You Could Be Better Off Than You Think, and How to Make That Happen*, and they argue that Canadians not only can, but for the most part will, achieve a comfortable retirement. However, to reach their goals they will have to rely less on government than previous generations did and replace that with personal responsibility for saving and investing for retirement. The good news is you don't need to replace 70 per cent of your pre-retirement income to maintain your lifestyle. According to Vettese and Morneau, the target is closer to 50 per cent. Their book catalogues post-retirement expenditures, emphasizing that consumption declines with advanced age. They break retirement down into three phases with very different financial requirements. Phase 1 of retirement is the active age of retirement when expenses are at their highest to support goals and interests people didn't have time for in their career. In Phase 2 people cut back on travel and other strenuous activities as their physical and/or mental capacities diminish. The majority of those who reach Phase 3 are in a nursing home, and most of these costs are covered by our national healthcare system.

Henry is 84 years old and would probably rank himself as transitioning from Phase 1 into Phase 2. Although his retirement income is significantly less than his working income, he has been surprised at how little money he needs to live well. "I wondered how I would ever live on my pension," he said. "But I live much higher than I expected. I'm particularly happy. It turns out that you don't need much. The sorts of things that are really important are not hard to find. You can always have a radio and a CD player and a public library. But you do need to think about this in advance and make some changes in your thinking. You don't want to be in a position where you feel hard done by financially. One does gets used to things, and it's far easier to get used to having things than to do without."

Getting the right kind of financial advice at the right time can make a big difference to your financial picture. One of the things Murray did that improved his finances was to hire a lawyer to provide him with strategic advice when he left his company. "He helped me think through what I could ask for and what was reasonable," Murray said.

When I interviewed Wallace, he told me he wished he'd received financial counselling when he switched employers. "My biggest mistake was not doing financial planning at the time of changing my job," he said. "I should have hired someone to advise me. My pension was very much reduced because when I changed jobs my pension was not transferred. I had done very little conscious planning about retirement, and I didn't focus properly on the financial implications of this move. The net result is that we live on one-quarter of our previous income. We now have to think through some things very consciously. We give less to charity, and our travel is done much more on a budget. The one thing we did well was to downsize to a more economical home."

The retired men I interviewed, like the majority of Canadians, do not appear to be in danger of outliving their retirement savings. In cases where their standard of living has been reduced from their working days, they are finding ways to economize and still enjoy retired life.

Health

Of the four dreaded Ds of retirement I was warned about, three of them—death, drink and depression—are components of men's health. Any attempt to connect retirement with these Ds is complicated by the fact that some men retire because of poor health, so retirement shouldn't be blamed for their unhealthy condition. Statistics Canada reports that almost 30 per cent of people who retired between ages 50 and 59 gave poor health as a reason. Men who rated their health as poor or fair were almost five times more likely to stop working before retirement age compared with those who perceived their health as excellent. As well, men who were heavy drinkers were almost twice as likely to exit the labour force early.[15] So if we're seeing a link between retirement and poor health or a tendency to abuse alcohol, we may be looking at men who retired because they had these problems rather than becoming vulnerable to these conditions post-retirement. As well, although worrisome stories circulate of people dying shortly after they retire, there is no reliable statistical evidence linking retirement with premature death.[16]

But aging does bring some chronic conditions such as heart disease, high blood pressure, diabetes, and conditions affecting vision and hearing. Eighty-nine per cent of Canadian seniors report at least one chronic condition, with arthritis and rheumatism being common, and many seniors are affected by a combination of these conditions.[17] However, the group of men I interviewed will most likely be in better physical shape in retirement than they were when working. The reasons are twofold: they are making healthy living a major priority, and they have more time to devote to their goal. They are running, biking, hiking, walking, swimming and working out, and generally determined to be in better shape than they were before leaving the workforce. Many of the men have scheduled fitness regimes, and some of them undertake major hikes or long-distance biking trips.

Some men told me they gave themselves a measurable fitness goal. Albert set himself a monthly walking distance target of sixty miles a month. "When things get busy, this target is often missed," he said. "Nevertheless having a target keeps it front of mind. A few years ago, I was given a warning which went something like this: 'Up to age 60 your body takes care of you. After 60 you have to care for it by staying active and fit.' When my son started gently poking me in the tummy, I figured it was time to lose twenty pounds, so I'm keeping away from the snacks and carbs."

Ryan told me that one of his retirement goals is to prolong his life—against family odds. "My father died at age 52 of a family heart condition," he said. "I had stents put in four years ago. Recently my cardiologist told me I needed to lose weight and get active. I said, 'Pick one' and she said, 'Being active is better.' I've started to work out and am going to the gym five to six times per week. I feel better and have more energy, so that's a big bonus. I find I don't have to force myself to go, which is a big revelation."

When I interviewed Gerry, he told me he was impressed by the experience of a friend who, at the end of his working life, had stress and health issues, but was able to get back in shape after he retired. Gerry is retiring in a few months and plans to have a full physical before beginning his retirement. "I'm going in hopes of getting a clean bill of health," he said. "One of my retirement goals is to spend time on my fitness. I used to coach tennis and hockey, and I'd like to get back to doing something physical."

One of the reasons Stewart went into semi-retirement was to improve his health. "Just before I decided to leave my full-time job, I had been in the hospital with kidney stones, and I generally wasn't feeling great. By becoming my own boss, I can go for a bike ride, work out with a trainer, and still be in my office by noon." Victor doubts he would be alive if he were still working. "After I retired, I was able to pay more attention to my health," he says, "and

I finally got around to having a check-up. That's when my GP found my cancer, and he saved my life."

Then there are the fears about drinking and retirement. In the interviews, men made numerous references to worries about becoming dependent on alcohol. So I was surprised when I looked at the data. Rather than people abusing alcohol more as they age, the figures show the opposite: the number of heavy drinkers decreases with age. The Canadian Addiction Survey found that most older Canadians drink in moderation, with 85 per cent of them typically having a drink or two per day. Only about 2 per cent are heavy drinkers. By way of comparison, nearly a third of people aged 20 to 24 are heavy drinkers and one in five of those aged 25 to 34.[18]

But retired men should watch their drinking, especially if they have a family history of alcohol abuse. In *The Stressed Sex*, Daniel Freeman and Jason Freeman examine the latest scientific and medical evidence on the role of gender on psychological disorders. They focused on studies of people under 65 and concluded that men are more likely than women to develop problems with alcohol. Alcohol disorders tend to run in families. So if a person's parent and grandparents have been dependent on drink, there's an above average chance that person will develop the same problem. According to the Freemans, the heritability of alcohol disorder is moderate to high at around 50 to 60 per cent. "What it tells us is that 50 to 60 per cent of the differences in rates of alcohol disorders across the population may be linked to genes, with the remainder caused by environmental factors."[19]

Several of the men I interviewed were aware of these familial tendencies and are taking steps to make sure they stay healthy. For Derrick a big motivator in finding meaningful activity in retirement is because he feels the social interaction and the routine will ward off depression and substance abuse. "It's all about why we work," he said. "I'm very alive to a concern about depression. I have friends who have fallen into depression, and this led them to alcohol or drug dependency. I have seen that happen in my own family with two of my brothers."

Bruce became proactive about his drinking when he found it getting out of hand. He was forced to take mandatory retirement before he was mentally prepared and went through a difficult period while coming to terms with his new life. "I found I was doing way too much drinking," he confessed. "But, in the past three years, I haven't had much to drink. Now I'm strong enough to just have a sip, and I don't want more."

Considering the warnings about the link between retirement and depression (another one of the dreaded Ds), I was surprised to learn older people are not at greater risk of depression than young adults. Approximately 10 per cent of the population suffers from depression, and the rates do not vary with age.[20] According to the Public Health Agency of Canada, the majority of seniors report they are in general satisfied with life and that they have very good or excellent mental health.[21] In *The Stressed Sex*, the Freemans report that depression affects roughly twice as many women as men, and is most likely to occur when a person who is vulnerable to the disorder finds himself or herself going through a stressful period, particularly if these stressful events involve humiliation or entrapment, and when social support is lacking.[22]

Dr. Ira Katz, a geriatric psychiatrist and authority on treating late-life depression, encourages people to take seriously any sign of clinical depression. The onset of any symptoms of depression should be discussed with your physician and evaluated for appropriate treatment. Dr. Katz's studies have shown that depression turns up the volume on pain, accelerates osteoporosis, and increases other symptoms of disease and ill health. "Everyone who works with older people is amazed by their ability to cope with disease, loss, disability—as long as they're not depressed," Katz says.[23]

I was curious about the role that depression and alcoholism played in Ernest Hemingway's tragic suicide at the age of 61. The prize-winning American author was the quintessential man's man, and I made the assumption that aging must have been difficult for someone who prized his testosterone-driven life of hunting, fishing, bullfighting, adventuring and womanizing. He had married four times, been in three wars and received a medal of bravery, and, at his 60th birthday party, shot a cigarette from the lips of a friend. But Hemingway was also the artist who had created Santiago, the formidable old fisherman in *The Old Man and the Sea*, which earned him the Pulitzer and Nobel Prizes for literature. In this 1952 novel, which Hemingway wrote in Cuba, Santiago has come in from the sea empty-handed every day for over eighty days. His peers view him as *salao* (having the worst bad luck), and the parents of his young apprentice insist he leave Santiago's boat and go out with the successful fishermen. "They sat on the Terrace and many of the fishermen made fun of the old man and he was not angry. Others, of the older fishermen, looked at him and were sad. But they did not show it and they spoke politely about the current and the depths they had drifted their lines at and the steady good weather and of what they had seen."[24]

When Santiago decides to try his hand far out in the Gulf Stream, he catches a monstrous marlin. He is alone with the fish and for days engages in a life and death battle, first trying to keep the fish on his line, and then fighting off the sharks who devour chunks of the marlin's carcass. By the time the exhausted Santiago gets home, the sharks have picked the marlin clean of flesh, leaving only the skeleton tied to Santiago's skiff.

When I first read this brilliant book, I had to force myself to keep reading, anticipating the wrenching sorrow I would feel when I reached the last pages. Tears well still when I think of the old man's determination. "I may not be as strong as I think," he says. "But I know many tricks and I have resolution."[25] As it turns out, these attributes aren't enough to land the big fish intact. However, they are enough to redeem his reputation. I wondered what had happened to Hemingway's own tricks and resolution.

Sadly, it appears that Hemingway was being proactive about his health just before his death, but it wasn't enough to save him. The injuries he suffered from plane crashes in Africa in his early 50s had left him in constant pain, the alcohol that had fuelled his writing had damaged his liver, and it seemed that suicide was never far from his mind. Reading Carlos Baker's biography *Ernest Hemingway: A Life Story*, I was struck by how frequently throughout his life Hemingway had talked about killing himself as a way of resolving a problem. When he received the news that his father had committed suicide, he apparently said, "I'll probably go the same way." Hemingway's good friend, the editor and writer A. E. Hotchner, published the correspondence the two had exchanged over decades and sums up Hemingway's sad end. "These letters demonstrate the chaotic state of his mind leading up to suicide. . . . I wept at the tragedy of Ernest's decline, the fact that he had committed himself to suicide, this man who had been so vibrant, so in control of his destiny, now a victim of his delusions."[26]

Some of the men I interviewed talked about mental health issues and sought help when they felt it was warranted. When Caulfield retired, he went through a legal battle with his employer and the process took its toll on him. "My mood shifts were really strong. I started drinking a lot, and I had medical problems for about six months. I stopped being myself. Now I am more on an even keel. But I'm still going through a period of self-examination. I went to a therapist for a while and that was a big help, but he eventually fired me. He told me I could use my time more productively in other ways."

When Chris began showing symptoms of Parkinson's, he heard about the link between the disease and depression. To be proactive about his condition, he enrolled in a university research study that explores the connection between Parkinson's and depression. When I interviewed Harold, he told me about a research project he was looking into that focuses on depression. There is a history of addiction and depression in his family, and Harold has been taking antidepressants for years. A medical facility near his home is conducting research to see if a daily dose of mild antidepressants will improve the lives of older people and Harold is monitoring the results with interest.

False Assumptions

Men are bothered by the prospect of becoming grumpy old men. However, this stereotype runs counter to the research findings that people get happier as they age, not gloomier. The surgeon and writer Atul Gawande discusses this phenomenon in his book *Being Mortal*. According to a study that tracked the emotional experiences of nearly 200 people over many years, people reported having more positive emotions as they aged. As time passed, they were less prone to anxiety, depression and anger, and found living to be a more emotionally satisfying and stable experience.[27]

Despite reality, the grumpy old man myth persists. We know popular culture loves this stereotype. The movie *Grumpy Old Men*, which stars Jack Lemmon and Walter Matthau, is a case in point. I wondered whether people's encounters with older men might lead them to form the mistaken impression that they were grumpy. And, if so, why. So I canvassed some older men, and we came up with some plausible explanations. For example, if an older man is losing his hearing, he might not respond to a greeting, or he might answer inappropriately, leading people to conclude he's in a bad mood. Or maybe someone assumes an older man is grumpy based on a sour expression on his face. But what the person sees could just be the effects of gravity. When the older face is in repose, sagging facial muscles often turn the resting mouth into a frown. When

I interviewed a 90-year-old man for *You Could Live a Long Time: Are You Ready?* and asked him how to live well at his age, he recommended I smile more the older I get, to counteract this natural tendency. In *Travels with Epicurus*, Daniel Klein talks about his "old-mannish smile" and muses that "perhaps people's smiles fall when they age because of bad dentures." He decides against getting what he calls "youth implants." "With my years of clear thinking and reasonable mobility dwindling as quickly as my jawbone," he writes, "did I honestly want to dedicate an entire year to regular visits to an oral surgeon? I did not."[28] And this leads to another plausible explanation for the stereotype—the complex and quirky sense of humour of the older mind. We older people enjoy the sense of irony and playfulness of the mature brain, but to the young untutored mind it may come across as mere grumpiness.

So, contrary to the fears, retirement does not automatically mean declining physical and mental health. And this holds true for aging in general. Some of the men I interviewed made assumptions that their physical prowess would have peaked at a young age, to be followed by a slow, or rapid, descent to the grave. This picture is inaccurate. Mental and physical capacities peak and decline at different points in our lifespan. And medical treatment and interventions have resulted in the graph of someone's health and performance looking like a series of valleys and peaks, with low points followed by high points, rather than being a smooth descent or a precipitous drop. When it comes to chronic illness, Atul Gawande says in *Being Mortal* that treatments can "stretch the descent out until it ends up looking less like a cliff and more like a hilly road down the mountain. The road can have vertiginous drops but also long patches of recovered ground."[29]

In my years of interviewing older adults, I have been astonished by the way procedures to improve their bodies' functions or repair their parts, such as replacing hips or knees, removing cataracts or treating heart disease, were able to rejuvenate people. When I interviewed Saunders, he found that at age 65 he had more mobility than he'd had for years, and, indeed, had ever expected to have again. "I was in a ski racing incident about twenty years ago, and I've had knee problems ever since. I was at the point of having to wear a brace. About six years ago, I finally had a partial knee replacement, and then two years ago they did the other one. Now I'm enjoying things I haven't been able to do for years, even something as simple as carrying bags up the stairs. I've started playing tennis again. My bad knees held me back more than I thought. I didn't realize I was avoiding doing so many things."

The question of longevity arose frequently in my interviews because I was asking men about how their fathers retired and about the way they pictured their own life course. When many men spoke about their lifespan, they were basing their assumptions on their family history. This can lead to false expectations because, as it turns out, only 3 per cent of how long you'll live, compared with the average, is explained by your parents' longevity.[30]

It's important for men to free themselves from negative thinking because of the importance of attitude on healthy aging. Researchers examined a group of people who experienced heart problems after reaching the age of 60 and found they tended to have been thinking negatively about aging from early on. Their episodes of heart disease could not be explained by common risk factors such as smoking, depression, cholesterol or family history. The researchers concluded that "age stereotypes internalized earlier in life can have a far-reaching effect on health."[31]

The power of age stereotyping is well illustrated by this story Peter tells about his friend Harry. "When he turned 40," he said, "he started referring to himself as 'Old Harry.' He became overweight, and smoked and drank too much. He died when he was 45. As far as I'm concerned, what killed him was the stereotype he had in his head about getting old."

When it comes to stereotypes about aging, it's hard to beat Jonathan Swift's grim picture of the Struldbrugs in his 1726 classic, *Gulliver's Travels*. The brilliant satirist created these unforgettable immortals who do not die, but they do get old and "pass a perpetual life under all the usual disadvantages which old age brings along with it. . . . They were not only opinionative, peevish, covetous, morose, vain, talkative," he writes, "but incapable of friendship, and dead to all natural affection, which never descended below their grandchildren. . . . The least miserable among them appear to be those who turn to dotage, and entirely lose their memories."

Swift's creations vividly reinforce an ageist world view, and I wondered about his own relationship with aging. He was 59 when he wrote *Gulliver's Travels* and lived until age 77, but he began thinking constantly about his death when he was 47. Leo Damrosch, Swift's biographer, cites correspondence in which Swift claimed that, from that age on, he thought of his mortality incessantly. "The reflections upon [death] now begin when I wake in the morning, and end when I am going to sleep."[32] He wrote his own obituary, *Verses on the Death of Dr. Swift*, which was published six years before his death. Sadly, his life at the end bore some resemblance to the old age he had satirized in the form of the Struldbrugs. Swift described himself as a shadow of his former self, citing "age, giddiness, deafness, loss of memory, rage and rancor against persons and proceedings."[33] Damrosch says Swift became increasingly irascible, possibly as a result of his advanced dementia, and for his final years he was cared for "like a newborn infant." At one point he was observed rocking himself and saying, "I am what I am, I am what I am."[34] One hopes this is a sign that Swift found some consolation in self-acceptance as he reached the fate of his Struldbrugs.

One of the dangers of falling into stereotypes about aging is that it becomes a self-fulfilling prophesy. If you expect old age will be a misery, you're less likely to use your resources to manage your health, illness and wellness— with predictable negative results. Clinical psychologist Barry McCarthy wrote *Therapy with Men after Sixty* with his wife and partner, Emily McCarthy, to provide a resource for professionals. They advise that "men who adopt a proactive approach, especially regarding behavioural health habits, and being an active involved patient, live longer, have a better quality of life, and higher personal well being."[35] This is where men may have something to learn from women. Women are more likely to consult their physician and be in outpatient psychotherapy, whereas men tend to wait until there is a crisis or to seek help at the emergency room. Men are more likely than women to be hospitalized for a heart attack, addiction or a mental health crisis.[36]

It's encouraging to see prominent men speaking publicly about the benefits of seeking help, and this may motivate other men to do the same. When author Neil Strauss interviewed singer-songwriter Bruce Springsteen, he asked him whether he had ever been in therapy. Springsteen admitted he had, and said it was one of the healthiest experiences of his life. He acknowledged it had been difficult to ask for help. He had grown up in a working-class family where seeking help was very frowned upon, and he didn't know anyone who had gone to therapy. As a result of his treatment, Springsteen said he has lived a much fuller life. "I've accomplished things personally that felt simply impossible previously. It's a sign of strength, you know, to put your hand out and ask for help, whether it's a friend or a professional or whatever . . . it helps you center yourself emotionally and be the man you want to be."[37]

The late Mike Wallace is another public figure who urged people to get treatment for their mental health issues. The American journalist and co-editor of CBS's *60 Minutes* suffered for years from clinical depression. However, it was not diagnosed until he was 66 years old. He hid his illness for fear it would be perceived as a sign of emotional weakness, but decided to go public on a late-night talk show because he thought there might be people watching who needed to know there was hope. "I think I am a wiser and kinder man for having been through clinical depression," he said. "I really do. That doesn't mean I've lost the edge, but I'm more empathetic, more careful about making snap decisions. I think I like myself better."[38]

When I interviewed Brian, he told me he never hesitated to seek help when times were tough. "When things got really bad, I had the guts to book myself into a psychiatric hospital," he said. "Then I was born again through three years of counselling. As far as I'm concerned, the key to a happy old age is to avail yourself of some opportunity like counselling to get to know yourself."

This is a good point to look at another myth: "You can't teach an old dog new tricks." As mentioned, the deeply imbedded stereotype is that once you reach a certain age you can't learn anything new. You become rigid in your thinking, and your behaviour patterns are set in stone. New understanding of the brain's neuroplasticity has proven this assumption false.[39] Research tells us you *can* teach old dogs new tricks; you just might have to work a little harder.[40] A research project funded by the US National Institute of Health found evidence that training allows people to maintain their mental abilities, and the effect of training persists for years. The study, which was called ACTIVE (Advanced Cognitive Training for Independent and Vital Elderly), assigned more than 2,800 participants ages 65 to 94 either to a group that would receive ten one-hour sessions of training over five to six weeks, or to a no-training control group. Follow-up ten years after the training found gains persisted for aspects of cognition involved in the ability to think and learn, but memory training did not have an effect after that long a period. So the men I interviewed who wanted to stay intellectually stimulated were wise, because it does appear that if you use it, you can keep it.[41]

In addition, it turns out that old dogs can teach young dogs new tricks. Research has found that some forms of intelligence peak later in life. Recent work by neuroscientists at MIT and Massachusetts General Hospital evaluated a battery of tests performed by participants aged 10 to 89. According to Joshua Hartshorne, one of the study's authors, "At any given age, you're getting better at some things, you're getting worse at some other things, and you're at a plateau at some other things. There's probably not one age at which you're peak on most things, much less all of them." The study found that the ability to evaluate other people's emotional states peaked in people's 40s or 50s, and the skill declined very slowly later in life. What the researchers referred to as "crystallized intelligence"—the accumulation of facts and knowledge—peaked in people in their late 60s or early 70s.[42] So older dogs may not have the processing speed of the young pups, but they have lots of knowledge, world experience and interpersonal skills to share.

One thing the old dog may be particularly good at is philosophical thinking. This may be good news for Terry, the retiree I interviewed who told me he is spending some of his time figuring out the meaning of life. Research done at the University of California, San Diego, found that a slower brain may be a wiser brain because the parts of the brain identified with abstract, philosophical thought are freed from the distracting effects of the neurotransmitter dopamine. As well, as the brain gets older, it learns to better allocate its resources.[43]

But in some ways, you're only as smart as you think you are. We know that mindset matters. A growing body of research indicates that the stereotypes we hold about aging don't only affect our health, they can affect our cognitive performance.[44] So if we've bought into negative messages about the mental capacities of the elderly, we're likely to confirm our own bias as we age. Let's take memory loss as an example. How often do we hear people mock themselves for "having a senior moment" when they can't immediately recall a name or a fact? In the 1990s social psychologist Ellen Langer and epidemiologist Becca Levy conducted a study to compare the memories of young and old Chinese and Americans, and found that the older Chinese had memory test scores that were similar to the younger Chinese. Among the Americans, on the other hand, there were significant differences between the old and young. Older participants who held negative stereotypes about aging had lower test scores, and the researchers attributed the differences to the effects of ageism on the older Americans.[45]

In the subsequent decades, research conducted by Langer and Levy and their colleagues has continued to confirm the harmful cognitive and physical effects of negative aging self-stereotypes. Levy's goal is for elders to recognize that ageist stereotypes operate in everyday encounters, and for elders to realize they themselves may be unknowingly engaged in these distortions.[46] As further evidence of the power of negative thinking, a study published in *Experimental Aging Research* found that when seniors between the ages of 60 and 82 took a series of cognitive tests, their results suffered if the researchers implied in advance that old age was associated with poor memory.[47]

When I interviewed Stewart, he told me that he recognizes the cons of being an old dog, but he also appreciates the pros—and he wouldn't trade down in years. "I've noticed ageism with some of the people I work with," he said. "They don't want to deal with the old generation. 'Old-school' is the worst thing someone can say. But on the positive, I don't get invited to workshops on organizational strategy because of my youth. It's my experience. I'm a walking encyclopedia, and I have lots of war stories. I feel very comfortable being 66. I work very hard at staying in shape—mentally and physically. I'm not decrepit. The only people I know who wish they were younger are those chasing after younger women."

To be reminded of the assets of age, it's instructive to spend time with Rembrandt's paintings, particularly his self-portraits.[48] Rembrandt van Rijn died in 1669 at age 63, leaving a legacy of hundreds of paintings and etchings, and thousands of drawings, many of them unforgettable works of genius. Looking at the self-portrait Rembrandt painted the year of his death, which hangs in London's National Gallery, you can see the travails of his life writ large. Here is a man who buried his two great loves and four of his five children, who was forced into bankruptcy and lost his family home and nearly all his possessions, and whose staggering talent was often overlooked in favour of his less inspired, more conventional students. Yet, for all that, we see a man unbroken, whose unflinching gaze encompasses all the sorrows of the world but also its joys. His face is the embodiment of that "crystallized intelligence" the MIT researchers identified in older people.

In his book *How Rembrandt Reveals Your Beautiful, Imperfect Self*, poet and writer Roger Housden describes the lessons we can learn from this master. He remembers seeing the self-portrait in the National Gallery for the first time and thinking Rembrandt looked sad, almost melancholic. But this gave way to a sense that there was both kindness and rigour in the gaze, all without a sense of self-importance. Housden felt he was receiving some hard-won wisdom from Rembrandt. "He was showing me who he was, and in so doing, he was showing me who I was. Resonance. Human being to human being. We are aging, we are dying, we are full of sorrow, full of feeling, full of life, we are beautiful however we look, we are who we are. That's all."[49]

Housden's story illustrates eloquently the dangers of the snap judgment when it comes to age. By spending more time in the presence of the senior Rembrandt's self-portrait, Housden realized he needed to rethink his initial negative impression of the artist as an old man. For his pitiable image, he substituted a truer picture of the depth and riches of the aged Rembrandt—a man in the fullness of life with so much to offer right to the end.

Timing

One of the critical factors affecting a man's ability to adjust to retirement is whether he feels he is leaving work on his own terms. The men I interviewed who felt the decision to retire was in their control found the adjustment easier, and research findings support their experiences. A survey of 1,500 retirees found that those who retired by choice had lower stress, a better quality of life and were happier with how they spent their time in retirement. They were more likely to be self-confident and optimistic about the future, and more likely to feel connected to the world, as well as feeling productive. They were also much less likely to be taking antidepressant medications.[50]

Some of the men I spoke to retired because they wanted to, others because they had no choice. And even those who chose their timing sometimes felt the circumstances didn't leave them many options. When I interviewed Albert, he told me that in his circle there are as many retirement experiences as men. "Several of my friends have been bought out and placed on pension even though they still had things they wanted to accomplish," he said. "In a couple of cases, men who were performing well and working on what they understood to be important projects inquired about retirement and found themselves out the door more quickly than they ever anticipated, with their 'important projects' left incomplete. Then there are those more fortunate individuals for whom retirement is a planned and agreed upon process—lots of notice given, a replacement hired and trained, and farewell on a mutually agreeable date. Even this happier outcome is, nevertheless, a huge transition."

Writer Esi Edugyan gives us a memorable image of the right way to leave one's work in *The Second Life of Samuel Tyne: A Novel.* "When your work is done, set it aside and forget it. Only a fool cracks a statue by continuing to carve."[51] While it's hard enough to recognize when your work is done, it can be even more challenging to negotiate your exit accordingly. When Hal retired at age 62, he knew that getting the timing right would be critical to his sense of self-satisfaction. "My last boss was incompetent and toxic," he explained. "If I hadn't had this boss, I might have stayed on for two more years. But I believe in self-determination. My business unit had a fabulous year, so I decided to leave with honor, leave with dignity. I really enjoyed my career, but it was like a meal, and there comes a time when the dinner is over. I kept thinking of Willie Mays. Mays was possibly the greatest baseball player of all time, but he played too long. Having the baseball bounce off his head at the end of his career meant that he went out with a whimper instead of a bang. He was an embarrassment to himself. I retired because it suited me."

For people like Willie Mays, whose work depends on their physical ability, changing capacity may dictate the timing of retirement. At age 58 world-renowned opera singer Ben Heppner decided to step away from the stage. Initially, he thought he would keep singing part-time, but found that being a part-time singer didn't work. "It's a full-time job," Heppner told the CBC. "No matter how often you sing, if you're going to sing at a good level, a quality level, you've got to keep it up all the time. And I was finding that to be a little bit difficult. So that, plus the fact that I've been experiencing a little bit of unreliability in my voice—and that causes some anxieties—I decided it was time." After retiring from his performance career, Heppner became the host of several CBC radio programs and took on other non-singing work including master classes, role-coaching and judging international voice competitions. "The best thing is to be remembered well," Heppner says. "I always thought it would be a cool way to go out on top. I'm not sure if I've done that, but sticking around just for somebody else's satisfaction just doesn't seem like the right thing to do."[52]

Some of the men I interviewed were willing to set their carving aside, to use Edugyan's metaphor, because they were leaving their workplace in good shape. In Albert's case being able to leave his team on solid footing was one of the primary reasons he retired at age 65. "Before I retired," he said, "I noticed my energy level was dropping, and I was starting to worry about being the boat anchor for my group. My two colleagues were the same age as my sons, and my manager was 40. Their minds were quick and they were more familiar with the new technology. At this point a chap was temporarily assigned to us who was really good at the job and got along really well with everyone. But we couldn't keep him because there was no opening. It was difficult to find someone with the skills and mindset to work in our area, and this was the first time we had a person who fit in so well. I wanted to turn my job over to someone of that calibre. So I announced to my boss that I would be retiring in a year, and I said, 'To build this team you need to keep this guy, and I can do cross training over the next year. We'd be a fool to let him go.' So everything lined up. I had the replacement and that chapter of my life closed. When an organization is at its peak, that's when you should leave. But, also, at the back of my mind was the fact that the men in my family are not long-lived and my dad had died at 76."

Gerry, too, is committed to leaving a legacy of a well-functioning workplace. He's 56 and has been working for the same company for thirty-six years. When we spoke, he told me he was preparing to retire in six months' time. Aside from his family and his boss, not many people knew. "I have a very deep connection with this place," he said, "and I want to leave things in good shape. There are three projects I started that I want to see well on the way. I have a strong desire to see my company do well and contribute to the Canadian economy and to my own pension. I know some people retire because they don't like their job. This isn't me. My boss is saying, 'What can I do to keep you?' I tell him, 'It's not about you, it's about me.' I have lots of interests that I want to spend time on. I'd like to have a music studio in the basement and do volunteer work with kids. My dad's death at age 37 certainly has a bearing on my feelings about doing these things while I can. The hardest thing about retiring will be leaving the relationships I have with my boss and the other team members."

Retiring so you can enjoy life while you're in good health was a motivator for many men, often because of advice received from friends in the medical field. "The head of surgery told me I better start thinking at age 60 about what I want to do," Barry said, "because the years from 65 to 75 would be my salad years. He said I was going to spend a lot of time after that looking after my health and spending more time with people like him." In my interviews I found this type of message to be particularly motivating for men whose fathers had died young. As mentioned previously, one of the reasons Albert was ready to leave work when he did was because the men on both sides of his family were not long-lived. "I wanted to be able to get out and enjoy life while I still had the health, strength and ambition to do so," he said.

For those men I interviewed who had the timing of their retirement in their control, it was usually a mixture of positive and negative factors that moved them towards the door. Often changes in their working environment made work less enjoyable and made retirement more appealing. Colin's work was quite specialized, and he had reached a point in his career where his routes for advancement were blocked. If he stayed, he knew he would continue to do the same thing, year after year. So, at age 56, he retired after working for the same employer for thirty-one years. "Early on in my career, I knew I would retire as soon as I could," he said. "I wasn't sure of the exact timing, but I planned to work only as long as it made sense. There were several factors in favour of leaving when I did. I had no room for advancement, I had reached the level where every extra year would not make a significant financial contribution to my pension, and I had a good replacement in place at work and no fear that things would collapse. Plus, work wasn't nearly as much fun as it used to be." After he retired, Colin did a bit of consulting. However, that gradually tapered off. "I technically still have clients," he said, "but I haven't done anything for them for years. And I'm not unhappy that I'm not doing more."

Clayton also retired at age 56 and was happy to leave when he did. "My last years were very tough," he told me. "My job required me to be front and centre all the time and I was beat. Earlier in my career, I had also worked day and night, but at that time I was really engaged and enjoying work. That changed. Just when I was getting ready to retire, my boss offered me a promotion. I asked, 'Is this really a promotion or just more work?' He admitted all he could offer me was more work and a fancy title, so I left. One of the reasons I was happy to go is that my employer no longer respected my team's depth of knowledge and experience."

However, not everyone is in a position to leave work when and how they want. Several of the men I interviewed experienced adjustment difficulties that they attributed to the way their jobs ended. When I asked Terry whether the timing of his retirement was in his control, he answered "yes and no." "I loved my work but it was extremely demanding, and I paid a very high physical and emotional price," he said. "During my last years of work, I was pretty burned out and I was really forcing myself to stay on. My stress levels were very high. I didn't think at all about what

I would do once I retired. The first months of retirement were a blur because I was still so tired. After I started to get my energy back, I found I was really missing the rush of work. I wasn't clinically depressed, but I was down for most of that year. I was able to replace a little bit of what I had at work by doing some volunteer work that made use of some of my skills. It was satisfying to find a way to continue to contribute to society. It was really the passage of time that got me out of it. Over time I've come to be genuinely and more deeply engaged in small pleasures, and I'm finding the same sense of enjoyment in little things that I did as a kid."

For Darryl, the timing of his retirement was doubly challenging. At the same time as he was wrapping up his consulting business, he and his wife moved back to Canada after decades in Europe. So he retired from work and from an entire way of life, both at the same time. "Planning and managing the relocation itself was just fine," he said. "I like big projects, so completing that gave me great satisfaction. What I didn't expect was the emotional hole at the end of it. It was really a question of 'is that all there is?' I tend to be proactive, so I went out to try to find new things to do. But I didn't have much motivation for anything. Upon reflection I think it's because I missed the old me. I liked the old me. What I began to fear was that I was going to find everything boring. And that got me into a real funk. I began to drink more and eat more and get into somewhat self-destructive behaviour. But then we went back to visit our old home, and I realized I didn't want to go back. I can't try and revisit the past. I need to go forward and do new things. But I'm still searching."

Caulfield is 65 and he retired three years ago. He feels the challenges he's been having adjusting to retirement were exacerbated by the way he left work. "It wasn't the ideal time for me to leave financially," he confessed. "My employer refused to allow me to retire when I wanted, and I spent a year with the union fighting for my rights, and I had to build my case. I was successful, but the battle really changed my transition to retirement and how it felt. I was tired of the bureaucracy and behaviour in the workplace. It had lost its gentleness and civility. So I thought it would be nice to have some free time but, once I had it, I didn't know what to do with it. So it's been a period of learning about my life and my raison d'être."

After Victor underwent surgery for cancer, he decided to retire. He was 60 at the time and he wasn't totally ready to give up the world of work. "I no longer had the will and mental state to continue working full-time," he says. "But I still wanted something to do. For me, work was pretty much everything: power, perks, prestige, friends, travel and, of course, financial compensation. It was really tough going from one hundred to thirty-five kilometres per hour in a matter of months. People stopped calling and went their own way." Victor is 69 now and would like to get back into the workforce. "It's tough to fill one's day with meaningful activity," he said. "I'd like to get something part-time with my former employer, but they won't return my calls. While I don't want to put on a suit and tie and drive downtown every day, I'm not ready to leave it all."

Some of the men I interviewed were still in the workforce but ready to retire and trying to get the timing right. Barry is still working at age 66 but keen to retire and waiting for the opportune moment. "It's critical to have it within your ability to select the time for retiring," he said. "I'm going to leave on my own terms. I have the option to work another four years, but I'm pretty certain I won't make it." What bothers Barry is that he's finding it harder and harder to get excited about work. "For most of my twenty-five- to thirty-year career, I worked with the same people," he said. "This meant that when I worked with them I didn't have much of a learning curve. And these were people that I liked very much. Now virtually all of them have retired. So I'm losing a lot of my community. Now most of my clients are a lot younger and they're wondering 'Why am I working with my father's advisor?' What's the fun in doing this? It's getting harder and harder to keep reloading the gun and go shooting for bear, harder and harder to get the same adrenalin rush. And the nature of the business environment has changed as well. It's a very different game, so the skills I have in my tool kit are not as important anymore."

Part of getting the timing right means getting your financial house in order, and this is a big factor in Barry's thinking. "I am probably the most frugal person you'll ever meet," he told me. "But I am long in assets. I need to get a bit more liquid. If I were to stop work now, I'd have a temporary lack of cash flow. Other than that, I could retire now. But you get comfortable." When I asked Stewart how he had been able to move from full-time work to semi-retirement, he said one of the key things was getting rid of the mortgage. "This gives us a degree of freedom," he said, "but it still costs us to run the house. I'm looking at every expense—like do we really need cable TV? But we live very well and there's certainly flexibility in our budget. Our biggest single expense is hospitality. And I'd like to find ways of combining more travel with work. But I've also saved money by not working full-time."

Planning

Self-help books place great store on the importance of planning for your retirement. But hardly any of the men I spoke to had given their retirement much thought in advance. Research finds their approach is the norm. Often, when people say they have planned for retirement, they mean they have thought about how much money they'll need, and not much beyond that. In one survey, only one in ten men claimed to have given a great deal of consideration to planning their retirement lives, and most of them focused on finances almost to the exclusion of anything else.[53]

Gene Cohen, the late professor of psychiatry mentioned previously, found that fewer than one tenth of his study participants, all of whom were over 60 years of age, had done any preparation for retirement beyond financial planning. He concluded that this lack of planning "undermines people's opportunities to broaden their horizons with novel recreational activities, educational enrichment, and civic engagement." Cohen emphasizes that a plan can be loose and open-ended, but it does require active exploration.[54]

There are good reasons why people don't plan ahead, aside from our shared tendency for procrastination and denial. As you've read in people's stories, retirement often comes upon people much more quickly than anticipated. And, while you're in the workforce, often the demands are such that there isn't much time or energy left over to explore other ways of being.

Linden MacIntyre's retirement from the CBC at age 70, after nearly four decades with the public broadcaster, illustrates one of the more extreme cases of leaving no time for retirement planning. The veteran investigative journalist retired in what he called a "spur of the moment thing" to take a stand against CBC's budget cuts, which he believed were having the strongest impact on young reporters and producers. He wanted to make room for them. In a radio interview with Shelagh Rogers some months later, he described the aftermath. "Before I knew it, I heard the click of the door behind me," MacIntyre said. "I suddenly realized I can't go back in there anymore. And everybody I know and everybody that matters to me is in there. What am I going to do? That's basically how it's been going since. So I'm kind of trying to get used to being on the outside not even looking in really, just on the outside period. And trying to figure out what I'm going to do with the little bit of time that nature seems to have put aside for me from here on." MacIntyre says he's going to continue to write. But he has always done that in the early morning hours. Then he would put on his jacket and go to work. "Now I have no jacket and no place to go. Sometimes I go to the gym. I remember reading a Kingsley Amis novel once called *The Old Devils*, I think, where old writers used to hit that point about mid-morning, and they'd gather in the pub. I don't think I'd last very long if I start doing that. So I have to figure out other things to do after I've finished with the creative process."[55]

People who go to bed employed and wake up retired have to do some on-the-job learning to figure out how to be a retiree. Ryan's wife has been retired for three years and she has been trying to prepare Ryan for what lies ahead.

"The first year is a holding pattern," she explained. "You're not so organized and you lose your way a bit. I've watched Ryan picking up interests and pursuing them for a bit, and then dropping them. At some point there will be a big dip that he's not expecting. My guess is, at one point, he'll get bored and he might get anxious. It's not dissimilar to what our teenage son is going through as he figures out the next phase of his life."

Ryan seems to be taking this advice to heart. "I'm resisting saying yes to things. I want to spend some time exploring. I don't want to leap into something unless I'm sure it's what I want. My perspective is shifting as I go through this process, so I'm allowing myself to take the time. Doing this reduces the anxiety of 'what will I do next.' I don't feel the days are empty. Just the opposite. I'm going through my parents' correspondence and shredding files. I have been volunteering with an organization over the years, and maybe I'll increase that. An acquaintance told me, 'I went into a funk for two years. All my contacts and friends seemed to evaporate. I no longer had that work structure. I only recognized I was in a funk after I'd come out of it.' Now my friend is thriving. I keep waiting for that funk to happen. But it may be too soon. I'm only just recognizing that I'm not on holiday."

Some of the men I interviewed prepared for retirement by having a practice run. They took an extended holiday or a sabbatical to "play-act" at being retired. In some cases the exercise persuaded them that retirement was the right next step, sometimes not. Regardless of the outcome, they learned about themselves and what they needed for the next stage.

Gerry spent a month at the cottage trying to imagine how he'll fill his day when he retires in a few months' time. "I got into a routine that was fitness driven," he said. "I really felt I wanted to get into shape. My wife and I would walk for an hour, I'd run for half an hour and then we would swim for half an hour. I started on a list of things I want to do, including organizing my papers, and realized it's going to take me a year to get through my list. So the trial was good. I didn't see any difficulties ahead for my retirement. I think I've got the physical side and the creative side covered by my activities, and the mental side I'm going to have to figure out."

Stewart took a sabbatical that was designed to revitalize him so that he could jump back into his work raring to go. It ended up convincing him he needed to quit his job and move into semi-retirement. "I had been in my job about 10 years," he said, "when I started showing all the signs of burnout. I had been working crazy hours and was very tired. I had difficulty putting sentences together and had a tough time staying focused, and staying awake. I've always said that I love my job. I just wish I didn't have to spend so much time doing it. I was 54 and I didn't have a pension, so I couldn't quit. But I knew I had to find a way to get a break, and I was able to negotiate with my employer for a nine-month leave. I loved my life on sabbatical. A sabbatical is supposed to make you feel more energized for your work and ready to dive into it again. But it had the opposite effect on me. I was even more committed to leaving, and I became preoccupied with what a wonderful life I had in my sabbatical. Still, I definitely felt better, and I stayed with my employer for another four to five years before I was able to figure out how to pull off my current state of semi-retirement."

Brendan took a sabbatical when he was 56, but in his case the time off convinced him he wasn't ready for retirement. After spending a year travelling with his wife, he returned to his job and is still working at age 60 with no plans to retire. "I'm a keen sailor," he said. "I decided to take our boat on a protracted voyage while I was still physically and mentally able. This would give me a chance to test out retirement and see how I would manage. A big motivator was that my dad had talked for years about all the things he was going to do in retirement, and then he died at 63. That's always bothered me. It was a big impetus for the trip. Well, I found running a ship was a lot of work. Up to then I'd had an executive job behind a desk. On the boat I became the mayor of our own municipality and it was a 24/7 job. The trip was highly successful, and my wife really increased her boating skills, doing multi-day and night shifts. I'm happy to say that we're still together, but she's done with boating.

"When I came back to work, I told my employer I was back to stay and I'd stay until work wasn't fun anymore. After being away from work for a year, I realized that doing nothing is not an option for me, and I wasn't ready to retire. I don't like gardening, and I don't want to organize my life around golf. My social life is around my work colleagues, and I like to discuss business issues with them. As well, my kids are back in school and back on the payroll, so I need the money in terms of cash flow. But having the sabbatical did give me a chance to think about what retirement would be like, once I do take the plunge. I've always loved working with my hands, so maybe I could make things. But I realized I don't want to manage employees again."

The next chapter looks at the many factors influencing men like Brendan to delay retirement.

Delayed Retirement

Reading reports put out by the financial industry, you run across the term *unretirement* to describe people who are working past age 65. But this word implies that such people are never going to retire. Given that most people will have some period of non-work at the end of their lives, the more accurate label is *delayed retirement*.[1] The number of men choosing to delay retirement is increasing rapidly. In 2014 about one in six men aged 65 or over was working, and this is double the number from 2001.[2] Looking forward, the number of working seniors is expected to jump again. When Ipsos Reid surveyed working Canadians ages 30 to 65, one in three of them predicted they will be working full-time at age 66, and an additional quarter anticipate working part-time.[3]

Some of those who delay retirement will eventually move to full-time retirement, others will transition to full retirement through semi-retirement, and others will have a period where they revolve between work and retirement, and back again.

In exploring what motivates men to delay retirement, I found a complex series of drivers. For one thing most men are conscious of their longevity. Current lifespan predictions give men an additional 18 years once they've reached age 65, and the men I interviewed, especially those in good health or with long-living family members, anticipate an even longer life. So one reason men are extending their working life is they can't imagine being retired for several decades.[4] Other factors having a major impact on delaying retirement for boomer men include the changing workplace, men's desire to work and their financial need.

Changing Workplace

Retirement-aged men are facing a workplace and an economy that are more accommodating to senior workers than in previous generations. Some men can work longer because there is no longer mandatory retirement in their workplace, and their employer cannot discriminate against them on the basis of age.[5] Some men are in non-ageist workplaces or in professions that value the contribution of older workers. Others are self-employed and set their own rules.

The later-in-life career of one of our friends is proof that age barriers are coming down. At age 65, he was offered a five-year appointment as a university administrator. At age 70, when he made his next career move, his new employer required another five-year commitment. The executive search team that headhunted him for the job admitted they had only recently introduced the practice of proposing 70-year-old candidates for five-year positions. These senior high-performers are proving that advanced years need not be a barrier to competency, and are forcing the workplace to evolve its thinking about what constitutes "over the hill."

And this trend will only increase as governments and employers focus on the potential economic contribution of the senior labour force. A UK report titled *The Seven Myths of Population Aging: How Companies and Governments Can Turn the "Silver Economy" into an Advantage* says that countries can avert economic stagnation by taking steps to increase the employment of older workers. A UK government study calculated that increasing time in the workforce by just one year per person would boost the level of real GDP by approximately 1 per cent. To do this requires addressing the incentives and systems that prevent older people from staying in the workforce, including pension provisions, tax systems and age discrimination laws. Researchers found that, contrary to expectation, greater workforce participation among older people was associated with greater participation among the young because of the increase in the overall economic pie.[6]

Increasingly, employees approaching retirement age are able to stand on the shoulders of those who have gone before them. Their older colleagues are establishing precedents for flexible hours or reduced commitments, and unions have negotiated agreements that accommodate the older worker. Manufacturers have been modifying their practices and procedures to support an older workforce, and the result has been reduced defects on the assembly line, decreased absenteeism and a rise in productivity. BMW found these results after making seventy small adjustments to its manufacturing process, including orthopedic footwear for employees and adjustable work tables. The physical changes to the workplace were made to reduce wear and tear on workers' bodies and lessen the likelihood the workers would call in sick. New wooden flooring together with weight-adapted footwear, for example, reduced joint strain, and the installation of magnifying lenses helped workers distinguish among small parts, reducing eyestrain and mistakes. The project is cited by BMW as a model of productivity and high quality, and the model, which originated in their power train plant in Lower Bavaria, is being rolled out to its other assembly plants.[7]

According to Michael Skapinker of the *Financial Times*, companies are going to have to accommodate older workers because the decline in the number of young people means retiring workers are hard to replace. And retirees are taking their experience and knowledge into ten- to twenty-five-year-long retirements. Skapinker says that Carlos Slim, the telecommunications magnate, is showing the way ahead by offering older employees a chance to stay on with his company and work only three days a week.[8]

In Canada the Workplace Institute acknowledges programs such as these through its annual award to the "Best Employers for 50-Plus Canadians" companies. The 2014 award winners include Sodexo Canada, a service company where over a third of the workforce is aged 50 or older. Sodexo's programs to attract and retain older workers include "reverse mentoring," where older employees share their knowledge with younger workers, and learn about technology and social media in exchange. The company has found that having a workplace culture that values older employees is good for business. Older workers score higher in employee engagement surveys, they stay longer, and they tend to be highly productive and loyal.[9]

Then there's the phenomenon that four out of ten older workers are self-employed.[10] This puts them in synch with the new on-demand economy, which favours the flexible.[11] Retirees looking to keep their hand in the workforce can operate through a company such as Handy, which connects people who need home help to service providers through its app; or Airbnb, which allows the retiree to host a B&B in his home and market to international tourists; or Uber, which could help him use his spare time to provide a taxi service. The online world offers endless opportunities for retirees to go freelance and make their own match ups.

Those with goods and services to sell can connect with customers through a vast array of online options aided by search engines, websites and social media. A retired computer programmer could provide virtual support to customers; a retired chef might use his website to sell custom wedding cakes; a creative retiree could turn an artistic hobby into a revenue generator. Examples are limited only by the imagination.

According to the Kauffman Index of Entrepreneurial Activity, the highest rate of entrepreneurial activity in the US over the last decade occurs in the 55-to-64 age group. About 20 per cent of all new businesses in 2013 were started by entrepreneurs aged 50 to 59 years, and 15 per cent were 60 and over.[12] The nonprofit organization SeniorEntrepreneurshipWorks.org was set up by a 71-year-old woman to help workers over age 50 start their own businesses. The Center for Productive Longevity holds conferences for people 55 and older who are interested in entrepreneurship as a way to remain productively engaged. Its national contest recognizes outstanding examples of later-life entrepreneurship to demonstrate that older people can remain productively engaged beyond traditional retirement age.[13]

If the equity markets are paying attention, they'll be rewarding senior entrepreneurs. UK research found that 70 per cent of start-ups founded by older people lasted longer than three years, in contrast to only 28 per cent of those created by younger entrepreneurs. There's even a label for this group, now dubbed "elderpreneurs," referring to someone aged 50 or over who owns and operates a business.[14] When Barclays Bank did a survey of business start-ups in England and Wales, they concluded that "entrepreneurs aged 50 and over are becoming a force to be reckoned with in the UK economy."[15] Grey entrepreneurs are more experienced, possess more social, human and financial capital, and face less stress because few rely on the business as their family's sole source of income. They also think more clearly about objectives and pitfalls, which may explain their better survival rates.

In the US, in addition to encouraging senior entrepreneurship in general, a number of organizations are focused on helping older people find work that helps them give back to the community. Groups like Civic Ventures and the Sloan Foundation support people to develop an *encore career*, a later-in-life career that combines personal meaning and social impact. When I interviewed Murray, he said he would like to see more attention paid to this issue in Canada. "I wish there was more encouragement for encore careers in Canada, the way there is in the US," he said. "There's an interest from we seniors, but not from the folks who should be sponsoring it, like governments or educators."

Love and Money

While society may be more supportive of men working past retirement age, why do men decide to keep working? According to Statistics Canada, about half of the people who returned to work after having been retired did so because they liked working or being active, and about the same number said they returned for financial reasons.[16] Financial necessity was what drove Nick Bacon back to the workforce. Bacon told the *Globe and Mail*'s Tavia Grant that he went back to work after having retired at age 67 because he and his wife didn't have enough to live on. Bacon is a former general manager of a road-sign company, and he found that his pension combined with his wife's didn't give them enough money. During the winter months they couldn't afford to go out, so they sat at home reading and watching television. In hopes of augmenting their income, Bacon invested in a vending machine business and has returned to a forty-hour work week.[17]

But for many of the men I interviewed, the issue is not as clear-cut, and their reasons for working can't be neatly categorized as being a case of either love of work or money. Many men are working because they need the income, but, happily, they like to work. Others feel they could survive without the additional income, but having it is a bonus that comes from doing what they enjoy.

When I interviewed Duncan, he told me about the

ongoing discussion he's been having with his son about retirement. Duncan is the apartment-building superintendent who's been working at his job for over thirty years. He's 88 years old and doesn't need to keep doing it for the money. His son has built a suite for him in his home and is trying to convince him to move in. But moving into his son's home would mean relocating to another town, and Duncan would have to give up his job. This option holds no appeal for him. "I like my work," he said. "Like all jobs, it has its good days and its bad days. I just try and do the best I can. I had stomach cancer and survived that. I have a pacemaker and I just had it checked out. The doctor said, 'You'll have another nine years on that one.' What the heck would I do if I retired? I'd probably just kick the bucket. I'll keep going as long as I have my health. If I see any deterioration, I'll pack it in."

At age 78 Gene is a serial retiree. "I have retired and gone back to work four times," he told me. "I like to work. Any time it's no longer fun to get up in the morning and go to work then I figure it's time to go someplace else. So I set myself a new challenge to develop a new career. My focus is maintaining a purpose for living. If you have no purpose, life loses its flavours. I work best when I'm creating something. For my latest project I'm creating a U-pick orchard. I'm planting 500 Saskatoon berries and 140 cherry trees. I've put in decks, a septic system, a garage and a bunch of sheds on the property. After the trees are established, I'll plant vegetables between the rows and donate them, or set up a stand on the side of the road. I grew up on a scrub farm, and I love playing around with the land. I'm back to where I started."

Parry is 66 and when I interviewed him, he told me he has no plans to retire—both because he likes working and for the money. "My need for finances is significant," he said, "and this works well with my proclivity to work. So there is no tension there. The way I see it, we all pull our ropes, and they all link to the tower standing. So as long as I have a rope to pull, I will keep pulling it. I'm going to be able to keep working, even with health problems, as long as I have the mental capacity. Maybe I would shift gears into giving advice or mentoring, but I would still be contributing. My mother is 97 and she was momentarily stopped in her tracks at age 94 when she broke a hip. Now, with her new hip, she's pleased because she figures she'll live another decade. I grew up with the model where you stop working only when you could no longer do it. I remember when I was in Grade 4, being shocked to watch the principal get a gold watch for retiring. It made no sense to me that he should leave something he was good at. It was a foreign concept and I thought it was silly."

Alastair is 64 and his goal is to work until age 70. "We need the money, but I get so much more from working than the income," he said. "Work is fun, exciting and intellectually interesting. The only reason I would quit is if I was fed up with everything, or was tired out and would like less stress. Then I might just organize golf tournaments." Alastair's wife understands why her husband has no interest in retiring any time soon. "Money is a real issue," she said. "We spent too much on the children's education. But even if that weren't the case, Alastair would still like to work. He finds work challenging. He's always dealing with people from a whole range of different backgrounds, and he finds that exciting. If he can't continue working with his current organization, he's going to find other opportunities."

That's what Patrick did. He is 72 and when he was forced to leave his place of employment because of mandatory retirement, he turned around and found another place to work. "I was healthy," he said, "I had energy, and I was working at the same level as I always had been. So I wanted to continue what I was doing. Every one of my clients came with me to my new employer. I don't think my previous company's mandatory retirement policy will continue because they are losing people who are really in their prime. The advantage of being a professional is you can always go out on your own. One of my former colleagues set up his office in his basement. He has a unique specialty and has never done so well. I see myself continuing to work for another five years, health willing."

People in many fields feel they are just reaching their stride around the historical age of retirement. When the legendary Scottish-born photographer Albert Watson was asked at the age of 72 whether he had done his best work yet, his reply was "Not by a long shot." Watson believes that photographers improve with age. "You're relying sometimes on techniques that you've learned, and then later on in life you're using those techniques to make pictures. And that's what transforms them sometimes, that's what makes them richer. Because you have that experience."[18] The world-renowned cellist Pablo Casals was another artist who felt his work continued to improve with age. Apparently one of his pupils asked him why, at age 91, he continued to practise. He replied, "Because I am making progress."

When I interviewed Peter, he told me that at age 75 he has no desire to stop working and his inspiration is the men who were high-functioning and making major contributions at advanced ages. "My attitude has come from the examples of people like Winston Churchill and Charles de Gaulle," he told me. "They were running their countries in their late 70s and early 80s. Jackrabbit Johannsen was still skiing when he was over 100. I move from one job to another, and I'm doing a lot of volunteer work. I'm continuing to do what I want to do. I'm trying to avoid falling into the stereotypes of old age. Because I'm still working, most of my colleagues and their friends are in their 50s. People ask me why I don't go out and play golf or curl. I tell them that I do plan to do that someday—when I'm older. I'm the oldest in the old-timers' hockey league, and I do notice that my strength and my speed are diminishing somewhat. Some of my bodily functions don't work as well as they used to. I have to take medication for my prostate and urinate more frequently, but it doesn't interfere with anything I do. I tell people, 'Just keep doing it but slow your pace.'"

Some of the retirement-aged men I interviewed saw themselves as unemployed and were fighting hard to get back into the workplace—both for love and money. When I interviewed Willis, he was actively pursing job prospects and hoping to land something soon. As mentioned, he is 72 years old and his goal is to find a five-year position. "Financially, I need to work," he said, "but I also like to work. Work has a revitalizing effect for me. I like difficult situations. I like the challenge. I like the structure and routine of working life. I like being part of an organization because I find people energizing, and I like understanding their cultures. I don't work best in isolation. And I'm always learning. I would only stop working if I was getting fed up or not at my best, or I was not able to give it my best shot."

Ted was in a similar position to Willis. It took him a year to find the job he was looking for, but the position he landed was just what he wanted. After having worked overseas for many decades, Ted found himself at retirement age with inadequate savings and no job. "I launched a job search after returning to Canada," he said, "thinking that I would be employed pretty quickly. No such luck." After a series of contract positions ended, he decided to teach English internationally at minimum wage while he kept up his Canadian job search. After a year he was able to locate an executive position in Canada, one that was a perfect fit for his skills. "The process was depressing," he confessed, "but I hung in there. It was good to do the teaching. I had fun and the feedback was very positive. It made me feel better. If I hadn't landed the job I wanted, I was going to buy a backpack, turf what I didn't need, and wander the world until I secured a job or funds ran out."

Then there are those who are driven back to work by financial need, but end up thriving in their forced employment. Singer, songwriter, poet Leonard Cohen is one high-profile example. When Cohen turned 60, he moved to a monastery and three years later became ordained as a Zen Buddhist monk. He never fully retired, but he had slowed down. At age 70 he found out that his retirement savings had been mismanaged, and by age 73 he realized he had to do something to fill his empty retirement account. Going on the road to perform was one of the few options available to him. According to his biographer Sylvie Simmons, this was not a welcome prospect. His previous tour had been such a disagreeable experience that it was a factor in Cohen's decision to leave the music business and go to live in the monastery. But Cohen recognized touring was not going to be any easier when he was 75 or 80 years old.

His international tour turned out to be an outstanding financial and artistic success. The critic from *Rolling Stone* called the Toronto performance "stunning," after confessing to trepidation at the prospect of a comeback show by a man who walked on stage looking "like he just stepped out of the Dick Tracy retirement home."[19] The tour was also a personal triumph. As Cohen said, "[Touring] really re-established me as being a worker in the world. And that was a very satisfactory feeling."[20] According to Simmons, Cohen hopes he'll still be touring in his 80s and that he has "no sense of or appetite for retirement."[21]

For many of the men I interviewed, a big motivator to stay in the workforce was the need (or desire) to financially support family members. Some of the men had children late in life, some have adult children who need help, and some have commitments from prior marriages. Others are providing assistance to parents or other family members. Men of retirement age are often referred to as being part of the "sandwich generation" because they are supporting both their parents and their children. But some of the men I interviewed could more accurately be called the "club-sandwich generation," because they are supporting their parents, their children and their grandchildren.

David is 66 and he had his children when he was in his 50s. He puts together business deals and would dearly love to get into a line of work that is less demanding, but hasn't figured out how to do that while maintaining his current income level. "I have young kids and these are very high spending years for them, so I need the money," he said. "I'm working in a business where the average age is probably 38, and most people in my office don't get beyond age 50 or 55. Only a few of us are in our 60s. I get asked once a week, 'When are you going to retire?' My answer is 'When they stop paying me.' What's preventing me from retiring is the rate at which people in my family spend money. I figure this will carry on for another ten years or so."

When I interviewed David, it was late in the evening and he was still at the office. "Why am I still here?" he asked. "I'm not really that much into working. There are always people here at midnight, but they are much younger. I have other people now who do the work, but the problem is they want me to review it at 9 p.m., when it's finally produced. And then I am working in a number of time zones. So the work is really 24/7. I'm never off the grid."

However, David knows that if he leaves his current job, he'll want to replace it with more work. "I like problem solving and working with people," he explained. "It's a great feeling to have a successful transaction. Replacing this will be a challenge, and I'll need to seek some other business involvement to keep me active. I'd like to keep working, but on some project of my own, not somebody else's projects. I would simply like more flexibility in my work/life balance. I'd love more free time to do simple things like build things, fix things, play golf, read a book. I do think there are a number of opportunities for me out there that would give me that. The problem is finding the time to track down the right one while I'm still working. I could ease out of this job, but it would be a relatively quick slide."

While the children David is supporting are young, the financial needs of people's offspring often continue into adulthood. This was the case for many of the men I interviewed, and many Canadians are in the same predicament. In the 2011 census, Statistics Canada found that 42 per cent of young people aged 20 to 29 were living in the parental home. And even after they're launched, things happen. Children become unemployed or get sick, their marriages break up or grandchildren have special needs. And, even when there is no crisis, parents may want to give their children a leg up—to purchase a home, go back to school or launch a new career. When I interviewed Harold, he told me that every one of his adult children recently needed financial support, and all of them are in their late 40s.

Lawson is 65 and has started to reduce his working hours, but he has no intention of retiring completely because of his children's financial needs. "I could stop working and still manage my financial commitments to my ex-wife," he said, "but I want to continue providing support to my children. I like to help out my family, and you have to be making pretty good money to do that." Lawson's wife feels he is still working because he really enjoys it. However, he's also pressured by his financial obligations. "He supports so many people," she said. "He's supporting three families, plus us. This is a choice he's making, and one that I may not fully agree with. His adult children are not financially independent and we've had some counselling because 'enabling' is an issue. It's a hard thing to stop. The children are finally starting to become more financially independent, and over the next year or two we should be down to normal parenting. If Lawson could ever learn to say no, he could retire, and that is the truth. He doesn't want to, and I can understand that. He gets a lot from work. He needs to be accomplishing something to be happy with himself."

The life of Charles Dickens reminds us that working to support your family while in your senior years is not a recent phenomenon. Dickens was born in 1812 and worked until he died at age 58, a ripe old age considering the average life-span in those days was 40. He had ten children and became estranged from his wife after twenty-two years of marriage. Although we know Dickens as a brilliant and extraordinarily prolific author, he made more money doing public readings than he did from book sales. According to his biographer

Claire Tomalin, Dickens continued to do readings despite severe health problems, including a strenuous tour in the United States, because he had to earn money to support all his dependents. Dickens wrote a letter complaining of having to pay his wife's income and bemoaning that his sons had "a curse of limpness on them." "You don't know what it is to look round the table," Dickens writes, "and see reflected from every seat at it (where they sit) some horribly well remembered expression of inadaptability to everything.'" As well as incapable sons, there were needy sisters-in-law and orphaned nephews and nieces, and even his son-in-law was unable to earn a living. It didn't help that he'd fallen in love with actress Nelly Ternan when she was 18 and he was 45, and he felt obliged to support both her and her family.[22]

Renegotiating Your Job

Rather than stopping work abruptly, some men transition into retirement by negotiating reduced work demands. Smart employers appreciate that their senior employees are an investment, and know that replacing their corporate knowledge and job expertise would be an expensive proposition. As discussed earlier, employers seem increasingly willing to modify workplace policies and conditions to accommodate their more experienced employees. When an older employee is willing to work reduced hours or adopt a flexible schedule at the end of his working life, there can be benefits for both parties.

When I interviewed Ben, who is currently working full-time, he talked about his goals for a reduced work week. He is 68 years old and when he reaches age 70 he anticipates cutting back to four days a week. "I work in financial advising," he said, "and there's no reason I won't be able to perform at the same level. The way I see it, as you get older you don't lose your wisdom and experience, and you still have your relationships. But you do lose energy. So barring a question of health or I start to lose my marbles, I'd like to keep doing what I'm doing and gradually reduce the pace."

Even organizations with mandatory retirement policies find themselves making arrangements with people who have specialized knowledge or a unique expertise. At age 65 Leonard negotiated a new deal with his employer that includes reduced hours with reduced pay, and he finds the arrangement is working for both parties. "I was facing mandatory retirement from a partnership. But there was internal pressure from me to keep working because I like being busy. Changing mental or physical capacities won't affect my ability to work for the foreseeable future. An older colleague told me that deciding when to retire was a question of energy, and I feel I still have enough to do my job. Money was a factor motivating me to keep working, but not a big one. I'm also doing some teaching and some consulting. Although I'm still doing some work, I feel I have retired. It's a question of degree. I anticipate continuing to wind down and finding other non-work things to do."

Gregory is 72 and instead of opting for reduced hours he took a different route with his employer. Several years ago he negotiated what is essentially a business development and marketing agreement. "My retirement savings are adequate, so I didn't really need the money," he said. "All I wanted from my employer was access to a secretary and a travel budget so I could give speeches and attend conferences. I've developed a unique area of expertise, and I have a knowledge base that few people have. I really enjoy my field, and I want to stay engaged. Plus I get a financial bonus when I bring in business. I've brought in a few major customers, so this is working well for me. There is really nothing much that would stop me from continuing on this path. I may try to keep it up until I'm 75."

When you own your own business, you have more leeway in setting your working conditions. Lawson runs his own company and at age 65 has decided to reduce his hours. "I'm on the Freedom 95 plan, but my wife told me I was going to have to start taking more time off. So I work a shorter week and take time off in the winter. Once I got into the routine, I found it was working. So I feel I can continue my semi-retirement well into the future." Lawson's wife told me she is happy he's still working because it's good for him, and she is pleasantly surprised he's adapted so well to a slower pace. "He gets a lot from work," she told me. "He needs to be accomplishing something to be happy with himself. On his day off, the first thing he does is make a to-do list of what he wants to accomplish in the day. His attitude to work is partly his Type A personality and partly the way he was raised. He always did chores around the house from a very young age. He's a doer and has always been self-motivated."

Malcolm is 83 and I interviewed him at his office, where he continues to work in the medical field. With the support of his employer, he has been able to transition from patient care to information sharing, research and teaching. "These jobs keep me in touch with what's happening in my specialty," he explained. "It's a fast-moving field and it's very difficult to keep up. There's been an explosion of knowledge. Some colleagues couldn't wait to retire. What do they do? Some of them do decline when they retire. There should be no retirement except for those who are unable to work because of illness."

As employers increasingly appreciate the benefits of accommodating senior employees, men will find greater support for renegotiating their working conditions. By the time Albert was ready to retire, his employer was starting to offer more flexible work options, but the changes didn't come soon enough for Albert. "I spent five years requesting to work a shorter work week with longer work days," he said. "My commute time was an hour each way, so that change would have given me more personal time. Finally, on my last day of work, they offered me a part-time position. If they'd made this offer earlier, I might have stayed and worked more years. That's only a 'might.' But maybe others will be able to benefit from this option."

Reinventing Your Job

Some of the men I interviewed are using retirement as an opportunity to reinvent their work. In some cases they set out deliberately to forge a new career, in other cases new and unexpected job opportunities landed on them.

Saunders is 65 years old and is an example of someone whose new working life fell into his lap. When I interviewed him, he said he was completely surprised to find himself working again after having retired at 60. "My decision to retire had been quite sudden," he said. "I had been in my job for seven to eight years, and I was finding the work more and more irritating. I was frustrated with the red tape and the politics, and I was spending half my time putting out fires. Those things start to wear on you." As a result of his frustrations, Saunders ended up quitting sooner than he intended. "I didn't really plan it out," he explained. "I had thought I would work until 62, and all our personal budget numbers were worked out to then, but I decided I didn't want to wait. My wife wasn't worried because we had done a fair amount of financial planning, and we knew we would be okay."

Saunders really enjoyed being retired. He liked having a break and clearing his mind. He did a few little projects so he wouldn't let his brain go stale. Then two years ago he was approached to be an expert witness in his professional field. "This is a funny little niche and one for which I have the perfect background," he said. "What I like about this job is you have to focus. You read a lot of documents and distill the essence and present it to a judge. What's great about this way of working is it lets me concentrate on the things about my profession I like. Unfortunately in most jobs, the part of the work you dislike becomes more and more of what you do. As long as I can do the essence of what I like, my profession makes a good hobby. But a problem has been developing with this current gig—I'm starting to work too hard. I want to cut back to doing only a couple of cases per year, just enough that it doesn't interfere with my life."

When Andy switched careers, he opted for something completely different from his previous work. Andy is 66 and he and his wife purchased a hospitality business when he was 53. "Instead of asking myself how I was going to handle retirement," he said, "I was always wondering how to handle the next career change. Baby boomers have been forced to think that way. This was fine with me because I'm an entrepreneur." Andy and his wife phased in their transition, moving gradually from their former careers to focus full-time on their new business. "When we first moved up here, I continued my consulting practice. But I was starting to phase down," he said. "After I turned 50, I had already become more selective about my clients. My criteria was who I wanted to spend time with and less emphasis on making money. One way or another I knew there was going to be a career change."

In Andy's case the goal was to find something that worked for both him and his wife. "Running a business was the one career move that had the cross-over capacity where we could work together," he explained. "It was far enough removed from our previous employment to give us both the change we wanted, and we both had the needed skill sets. New didn't scare either of us. We needed to supplement our savings, but we didn't have to have a steady paycheque. Having been an entrepreneur all my life, I wasn't going to stop now." I asked Andy when he was going to retire from this job. "Only two things would stop us running our business," he said. "The first is if one of us dies, and the second would be a mental issue, which could also be a change in attitude."

When I interviewed Derrick, he was in the process of making a complete career change. He had retired a few months earlier at age 65, and his goal is to get back in the workforce as fast as possible. "It's only been three months since I left work," he said, "and I'm already going out of my mind. I had a list of projects and they're all done. If you know how to manage your time, you're going to get bored really fast in retirement. I don't have a lot of casual interests or hobbies. My wife's vision was that I would take cooking classes and become her personal chef. That isn't going to happen."

Derrick retired because he wanted a change. "I've been doing the same job for over thirty-six years," he said. "I retired because I could, and because I wanted to. For many years I loved my work, but over time it changed dramatically and got kind of boring. Now a lot of it is just busywork. Going through my files I realized how much of my work consisted of stuff I really don't like to do."

Derrick has been preparing himself for reinvention. "I've been attending night school at a technical college for the past three years," he said. "I just graduated and I have my degree. I want to go back to the work I did when I first graduated from university, four decades ago. I don't care about the money. I just want to get back to where I was then—being paid to work on my hobby. It's a technical field and there have been a lot of changes. I'm in the job search, but, so far, I've been unsuccessful. If I can't find anything, and I find I absolutely have to do something, I could always go back to my former job. But that would be an admission of failure, because I really want a change."

Derrick described his efforts to make himself attractive to employers, strategies that will be familiar to people trying to make a late-life career change. "I need to design a resumé that hides the fact that I'm 65 years old and I don't have any recent experience in this field," he said. "One of my college instructors has lots of connections in the industry, so I have been sending out CVs to these people. But I've had only one interview so far. I think they dismiss me as crazy. They have a great deal of difficulty understanding why someone who had a successful job would chuck that and come and work for them. It's tough getting taken seriously. They probably wonder how long I'm going to last. Also, I am kind of aggressive. I need to tone that down. These young managers do not want to bring in some older combative person. So I have to find a way to put that aside. I think I've created a lot of comic relief. I could start my own company, but then I would be owner/manager, and it's not what I want to do. I want to be back to the job I had forty years ago."

When Derrick was telling me about his job search, he said he felt like Kevin Spacey in *American Beauty* when Spacey was being interviewed for a job as a fast-food server. In the 1999 film, Kevin Spacey plays Sam Mendes, a 42-year-old husband and father who is having a major mid-life crisis. In the movie Sam is fired from his job at a media marketing magazine by Brad, the efficiency expert who decides he is expendable. As he works through his existential crisis, Sam says he feels as though he's been in a coma for twenty years and is just waking up. He looks back longingly to his youth when he was "flipping burgers all summer just to be able to buy an 8-track. . . . I had my whole life ahead of me," he says. When he sees that Mr. Smiley's fast-food restaurant is accepting applications, he requests an interview. The interviewer, a young employee, tells him, "There are no jobs for manager, just for counter." Sam replies, "Good, I'm looking for the least possible amount of responsibility." When the interviewer says he doesn't think Sam will fit in, Sam shows him his CV and says, "See, I have fast-food experience." The interviewer points out that was twenty years ago. Sam's reply: "I'm sure there have been amazing technological advances in the fast-food industry but surely you must have some sort of training program. It seems unfair to presume I won't be able to learn." Sam got the counter job and he liked it. When someone asks him, "How are you?" He answers, "It's been a long time since anybody asked me that. I'm great."

When Derrick told me he identified with Sam's employment search in *American Beauty*, he wanted me to understand he wasn't looking for a fast-food job for himself. "That would be way too high stress," he said.

Although many of the self-help books on retirement emphasize re-invention, most people end up doing some kind of work that bears some resemblance to their former jobs. As Derrick is finding, redesigning your working life requires dedication. But reinvention has a very real appeal for some people, and where there's the will, there's usually the way.

Relationships with Others

When men retire, they worry about what's going to happen on the home front. Four out of five retirement-aged men are part of a couple, either married or living common law.[1] Other men, although they live apart from their partners, may consider themselves as being part of a couple. Men are right to think about these primary relationships because they will be affected by their retirement.

When couples are given counselling to prepare them for the man's retirement, the following exercise is sometimes part of the package. The counsellor hands both parties a piece of paper and says, "I want you to estimate what percentage of time you will spend together after hubby retires, and how much time you each will spend pursuing your own interests. Label the time together 'we' time and the time apart 'me' time. Complete the exercise without consulting with your spouse, give the estimates privately to me, and I'll discuss the results with you later." When my husband and I were given this exercise, I laughed because

I'd already done some reading on this. "Let me guess," I said. "The estimates show that men and women are at polar opposites, with men predicting 'we' time at 70 per cent of their time and women putting it at 30 per cent of theirs." The counsellor smiled and replied, "It's usually not quite that extreme, but you're not far off the mark." The marketing research company Environics found that 54 per cent of boomer men say that spending time with their spouse is their top social priority for retirement. Only 38 per cent of women say the same thing. Women are twice as likely as men to name children and grandchildren as their main social focus in retirement.[2]

This exercise is popular in retirement counselling because it can reveal a fundamental disconnect in the way the retiree and his spouse see their lives unfolding, post retirement. Understandably, in solid relationships, the man may be looking forward to spending more time with his wife.[3] From his perspective the specifics of how their days will play out may be vague, but he assumes that the two of them will work out a new life together. He may understand that his wife has commitments and, in some cases, she may still be working. However, he assumes this new stage of life will be more about "us" and "we" than his working life was. For the spouse's part, while she may acknowledge that the vision of togetherness is romantic and endearing, she may fear that her satisfying life of interdependence with her husband will be replaced by a stifling dependency.

In Japan the custom has been for men to spend little time at home until they retire, and the Japanese language reflects the impact on the home front. Men who suddenly start hanging around the house are called *nure ochiba* ("wet fallen leaf"), a phrase that evokes the image of a busy housewife trying to brush her husband away only to have him cling to her broom.[4] Another even more uncomplimentary label is *sodai gomi* ("oversized trash"). Given this attitude toward retired men, it's not surprising that there is also the term *kitaku kyofusho*, which refers to a phobia of going home and being confronted with one's wife.[5]

The stress a woman feels because of her mate's retirement has been labelled a medical condition termed "retired husband syndrome" (*Shujin Zaitaku Sutoresu Shoukougun*— translated as "One's Husband Being at Home Stress Syndrome"). RHS is diagnosed in cases where a woman exhibits signs of physical illness and depression as her husband reaches, or approaches, retirement. Women are encouraged to receive therapy for their condition, while their partners can join one of the thousands of support groups that have been organized to "retrain" retired men to be more independent. The group called Men in the Kitchen, for example, teaches men to shop, cook and clean for themselves.[6]

When I interviewed Ralph, he told me he has relatives in Japan, and figures Japanese men would have a tough time with retirement because they are so defined by their work. "When I was staying with my cousin, I wanted to visit a couple in Tokyo I had met previously," he recalled. "But the man had lost his job and had turned into a complete recluse. When my cousin spoke with his wife, her husband wouldn't even come out to greet him. This was a guy in his 40s who had been a very outgoing guy, very skilled, who had been trained abroad. I would have thought he would have had more capacity to survive this. But he had been defined entirely by his job. He lost his job, so he lost his life."

If we consider the "wet fallen leaf" in the way the metaphor was intended—the retired man trying to re-enter his wife's domestic domain after years of absence—we sense it is already out of date in North America. In many households both spouses are working and the home is becoming much more shared territory. But at the root of the image lies a profound fear that is widely shared here by both retired men and their spouses. The man worries, "Will I be able to create a new life for myself, post retirement?" And the spouse adds the corollary: "And if he doesn't, what will that do to my life?"

Some of the men I interviewed who continue to work full-time post-retirement age understand these fears about being a *nure ochiba*. They admitted that their wives were happy with the status quo and not encouraging them to quit work any time soon. Ben said, with a laugh, "There's no pressure from my wife for me to retire. She basically doesn't want me around the house." His wife is retired and has a busy life that includes occasional paid work and a daily commitment to her horse.

Barry has been getting a similar response from his wife. They've been talking about his retirement, at which time they plan to move to another city. "The closer we get, the more she seems to have second thoughts," he said. "I know she's worried about what life will be like with me when I am around so much more. She has a full life. She sings semi-professionally, and she paints and does her own weaving and spinning. When the kids were still at home, I went through a period when I had a job with more reasonable hours. I'd even get home in time to take the dog to the park before dinner. The kids would say, 'Dad is around too much and gives too many opinions.'" He added with a laugh, "So my wife has a sense of what's to come."

Research confirms that wives are justified in worrying that their lives could be disrupted by their husband's retirement—but only in the short run. In the long run, men get better at retirement. The research found that when men first retired, they expected their wives "to alter their daily patterns to satisfy their personal needs. . . . Our survey further showed that wives often did no such thing—these men tended to complain that their wives didn't spend enough time with them." But over time most men adapt. They learn to either establish their own personal interests, or just accept that their wives have their own lives.[7]

Some men are quick learners. When Stewart left full-time work to set up a home-based consulting business, his wife was already running her own business from their house, and had been doing so for decades. Her office is spacious and large enough to accommodate the part-time help she regularly employs. Stewart's office is separate but adjacent. Here's how he describes his first day of retirement. "It was Monday and I slept in a bit. Then it really sunk in that I didn't have to go to the office. I was elated. I headed downstairs and into my wife's office to greet her, saying, 'Can I make you breakfast?' And then I noticed she was on the phone. She motioned me away. A few hours later, I tried again. 'Can we go out for lunch?' and she did the same thing. Later that day I asked about drinks and dinner. She replied, 'You've been bugging me all day. Is this what it's going to be like?'" He laughed, "Let's just say, I got the picture." When I talked to Stewart's wife, she gave me her version of the adjustment. "I'm sure Stewart told you his story about his first day of retirement when I said, 'Can't you just leave me alone?' It's a great story. But the truth is, the transition really wasn't challenging. We have both been self-employed at other stages of our work life, so it wasn't a foreign thing to adjust ourselves to both working from home again."

It took Hal a bit longer to make the transition, but then he was going from full-time work to full-time retirement—overnight. "My wife and I have been married for twenty-five years and we have a strong foundation. But we went through a bad patch right after I retired," he confessed. "A big factor was the abruptness. I opted to retire quite suddenly at age 62, partly in reaction to having an incompetent and toxic boss. Money was not an issue, but my wife had initial anxieties about our finances because she didn't have a reference point. She also worried about how our lives were going to change. She hoped I was going to have some structure to my life, and she didn't want me to follow her around. But I floundered for the first six to eight months. Things weren't in focus. I was watching too much TV and had no personal growth. My wife needed space, and I needed to get out of the house. I knew I needed to find my own space."

Hal has been retired for eight years now and is pleased to report that he's found his way. "I can now say that my wife and I have managed to pull retirement off with great success and pleasure." As for Hal's wife, she doesn't remember the rough patch lasting as long as Hal remembers. "Initially he was hanging around the house and watching me and driving me crazy. But that only lasted a few months. Then by word-of-mouth he got involved with several volunteer activities. It was a very smooth transition, and I didn't need to get involved. Now he is probably the busiest retired person you'll ever meet. My husband will never be bored. Not like my friend's husband. When my friend plays bridge with me, her husband sits at home waiting for her to come back."

Whose Home Is It?

When the man begins to spend more time at home, there is usually a shift in responsibilities in the domestic sphere. In some cases the overarching question—often unspoken is— *who is in charge?* The power struggle may show itself when the man decides to re-organize space or redesign procedures without consulting his partner. There are jokes aplenty about this dangerous course of action. Barry described a cartoon on this topic that made a big impression on him. "The caption reads: *Why do so many men die within a short time after retirement?* The drawing shows a man holding a clipboard and looking at a slew of productivity graphs plastered all over the fridge. He is saying, 'I've only been retired for three months and I've already figured out how to make things around here 40 per cent more efficient.' Behind him stands his wife holding a frying pan over his head, poised to strike."

Andy told me a true story that echoes this cartoon but involves a more strategic (and less violent) wife. "My

father-in-law had been the head of ordering for a car man-
ufacturer, so he was big on logistics and systems. He'd only
been retired for a few days when he told his wife, 'I'm
going to do some re-organizing around here. For example,
the pots and pans shouldn't be where they've been for the
past thirty years.'" I asked Andy how things worked out.
"My mother-in-law was a homemaker from the *Leave It
to Beaver* era," he said, "and one of those women who are
masters at letting the man think he's in charge. So she had
him fixed up with a list of assignments faster than he could
open the cupboard."

And then there are the tussles as the man carves out a
physical space for himself. He might meet granite-hard
resistance, as in this story told by Patrick. "On the first
day of the rest of his life, a man I know prepared a big
breakfast, set himself up in the kitchen with his paper,
phone and cigar, and spent the morning there. At noon
his wife slapped a sandwich in front of him and said, 'This
is my kitchen, my home. You need to find some place else
to go.'" When I told this story to my friend, she joked, "I
think I just met her husband. I was in Home Depot and
got great advice from a salesman about the changes we
were making to our bathroom. When I praised his level
of knowledge, he said he had been a plumber for years.
He added, 'After I retired, my wife sent me off to work at
Home Depot. She calls it my 'adult daycare.'"

But in most cases, the husband is not turfed out, and the space allocation is much more fluid and up for negotiation. Ryan and his wife were both working full-time until the demands of caregiving for an elderly parent stretched their lives too thin. "My wife and I talked about retirement at length because she was fretting about her mom. I told her, 'You'll kill yourself if you stay working when your mother needs you.' We discussed whether we should retire at the same time. I urged her to retire first and get herself established. So she retired four years ago, and she did establish herself," he laughed, "in the nice, bright computer room. And now I've retired and what's left for me is the man cave in the basement—the dark, mouldy basement, I might add."

Ryan's wife reminisces about the old days. "When it was just me in the house," she said, "it was heaven. I took the only good place in the house for my office. Now that Ryan is home I might switch rooms with him. But he likes to play music and spread everything out—and, in truth, the basement is the best place for that." Ryan's wife is back working part-time, and some weeks it's almost full-time. "When it comes to sharing the home space," she said, "I only have two rules. If we speak to each other, we have to be in the same room. And I don't want to have lunch together. Breakfast and dinner are enough."

Albert's wife has worked part-time for most of their thirty-eight years of married life and has no plans to stop any time soon. In addition to her job, she is an artist and her art provides a big part of her social life. When Albert retired a year ago, she worried about the impact on her life. "He is such a social animal, and I was worried that he would interrupt me all day long. I need a lot more personal space and some down time to recharge my batteries. As it turned out, I didn't need to worry because he's extremely busy. He has latched onto his retirement responsibilities and attacked them as if he were still working. He has things planned four times a week. It really helps that we each have our own rooms in the house—mine designed for my art and Albert's for his hobbies. These rooms have been our own designated spaces ever since we moved into this house thirty-six years ago. So the pattern works well for now and it's not the horror story I feared it would be. After I retire I don't know whether things will continue to work as well. I may go squirrelly."

Albert is also happy with the way things have worked out on the home front and realizes that having separate spaces in the house, each tailor-made for their activities, has been key. But his space and his wife's are side by side, which does raise a problem. "My only issue is my wife sometimes wants to have on background noise when she's doing something more routine. And, from time to time, I need to be so focused on the task at hand that I cannot abide any distractions—even music. So we have to work that one out."

In contrast Wallace and his wife have found they're managing very well sharing an eight-foot desk with two chairs. He is 71 and has been retired for two years. "Wallace does 90 per cent of the cooking and the grocery shopping—much more than his share," said his wife. "He's good at it, he likes to eat, and I don't like to cook. I've always been the one who's done all the finances and the one who writes emails, but he's very good on the phone. Where I draw the line is becoming Wallace's secretary and managing his calendar. At work he had a whole support team that took care of his schedule, and I don't intend to take that over. I think it's working out because I'd already been retired for years before Wallace retired." Wallace explains that his wife retired when a job opportunity for him meant a major move. "Me taking the job here meant she had to give up her job," he said. "So we decided to treat my job as a joint project and, in such cases, spouses never get recognition. So our vision for retirement was that we would do things that were mutually satisfying, and we've largely succeeded in doing that."

The car may also become negotiated space, especially when families have downsized to one car to economize around retirement. Albert's wife says being reduced to one car is working out so far because Albert lets her have the car and he usually takes the bus. She feels this is reasonable since she needs it for work. But in the case of Caulfield and his wife, who are both retired, they share the one car. "This means we're forced to operate a bit like the Bobbsey Twins," Caulfield's wife said. "Having another car would allow us to be more autonomous and let us each do our own thing."

Whose Jobs Are These?

For many couples household chores are a battleground, with studies consistently reporting that men aren't pulling their weight.[8] When men spend more time at home, will they take on more domestic duties? Ryan has just retired and already he's feeling the pressure. "I know what my wife's thinking," he joked. "Who's the fat guy in the kitchen? Why isn't he cooking?"

Many of the wives I spoke to said, indeed, their retired husbands are doing some or all of the cooking and have taken on other chores as well. Terry says that one of the benefits of retirement for him is that he has become a better cook. His wife works part-time and is an active volunteer, so he spends more time in the home than she does. She said, "Terry likes doing things around the house—he always has. He finds it very relaxing. Now that he's retired, he does it all."

Clayton has been retired for six years. He does about a day a week of consulting and manages the house. After he retired, his wife took on a demanding full-time job. She had gone back to school when their children were school-aged and had been longing to put her degree to use.

Clayton said, "It was her dream and her turn to have the opportunity. So for five years, I've been at home keeping the house tidy and being a house husband, and I've been as happy as a clam."

Murray is in a similar position to Clayton, having retired eight years ago to support his wife's dream of pursuing her career. His wife now works part-time and they have renegotiated their roles. Murray said, "I do most of the cooking now, but I'm not going to be the sous-chef. My wife and I made a deal that I cook what I want from beginning to end. I figure out what I want to make. I do the grocery shopping for the meal, and then I cook it. That way I'm enjoying it. I also do the laundry. But I tell my wife it will not be up to her level of perfection, and there will be no complaining. She can iron stuff she wants to iron. My motto is, 'Let me do it my way.'" Murray says he started getting interested in cooking through a men's gourmet club. "We hold dinner parties where the three men are the chefs and our wives are the guests, and we invite another couple to introduce them to the concept. The expectation is that we cook something unexpected and new. It's fun."

His wife said, "He now does all the cooking. He loves to do it and thinks about it in the morning and buys the groceries. He needs to make the meals he wants to make. He is a wonderful cook. I tend to restrict my cooking now to desserts and salads. I do not feel threatened. I used to be the one who paid all the household bills, but he's taken that over as well, and he manages all the repair projects I used to handle. Retirement has changed Murray. I would never have guessed that he had it in him to cook a tagine."

Support from Spouse

Having a loving partner can provide the retiring man with significant support through life transitions that are so major they make disagreements over space and chores seem trivial and petty.

Earlier I wrote about Caulfield's struggles to find equilibrium, post retirement. He credits his wife of thirty years with helping him find his path. "My wife is an amazing human being, and I love her now more than ever. A very positive aspect of our relationship is that we put our feelings on the table and explore them thoroughly. She has empathy and compassion and tries to see things from the perspective of the other person. This has helped me because I could have been reacting to my situation with anger, but now I have more understanding of the other's point of view."

Caulfield's wife has great empathy for him and is trying to be supportive without being directive. "The way Caulfield's job ended took its toll on him. I was worried about him. He was angry and depressed. He likes being liked and ended work in a way in which he wasn't valued. But I really couldn't help him. It was like a death, and coming to terms with it is a matter of time. He needed a couple of years to exorcise that bad experience a bit and realize his value. At first I tried to give him ideas about how he could become more active. I can't see a problem without wanting to fix it, but I can't really say myself what he needs. Marriage, like any relationship, is a compromise. We both give and get, or it doesn't work. As for the future, we are going to give each other space. But we need to keep checking in with each other about what we both need."

A supportive spouse is particularly important when the man's decisions around retirement appear risky, or when they focus more on the man's dream than the spouse's. As mentioned, at age 78, Gene has retired several times. As he explained, "What appears as work to some people was always fun for me. When it stopped being fun, I moved on to something new." So his wife had to be prepared to hang on for the ride, which is what she did. "We've been married for fifty-eight years and it's always worked out. One minute he was the director in a big job and the next minute he wasn't, and he didn't notice the difference. But for me it was the end of an era. He was only in his 50s and too young to retire. I asked him, 'Why would you retire?' He said, 'I'm tired of this job and I want to try something else.' When people said, 'What does your husband do?' I didn't have an answer. But I trusted Gene because every-thing always works out."

After that first retirement Gene started up and sold other businesses and is now on what he sees as his last project. "This time I'm riding into the sunset on a tractor and starting a U-pick farm. I am 78 and it takes about seven years for the seedlings to hit full production, but, hey, you have to be an optimist." Gene is very conscious that his wife's happiness is critical to his plans. "We don't do things independently. We are reasonably good at communicating and respecting one another's opinions. When I proposed this move to the country, she said, 'What if I get there and I don't like it?' I promised her we wouldn't stay. And that's a promise I'll keep."

Gene's wife knows she has the option to move back to their former home, which is being rented out until she decides. She confessed to me that she thinks she'll be happy staying in the new home, but she's keeping that to herself for the moment. "Gene's going along with anything I want because he wants me to be happy here, and that puts me in a good position. I think this is going to make a good retirement home. I never really cared for where we lived before. And Gene likes it here. He's planting berries and piling rocks. I think that's nuts. But I never say anything because it's what he wants to do."

Retirement often has a negative impact on income, and the spouse's willingness to accept a changed financial picture provides tremendous support to the retiree and gives him more options. When Stewart decided to trade in a high-profile, high-paying job for a life of consulting and semi-retirement, he saw it through his wife's eyes. "After I decided to quit, I couldn't bring myself to tell her for a few days," he said. "I saw it from her perspective. She's thinking, 'It's a great life we have right now. When people ask what my husband does, how do I explain he's at home now?' I overheard her talking to someone on the phone, and she said her anxiety level was up. 'I'm going to have to start pedaling harder,' she said."

As Stewart's wife remembers it, his decision didn't come as a total surprise. "When Stewart makes a decision there is a lot of internal processing," she explained. "Then he gets to the point where it's time, and then things happen quickly. I knew something had to give because he was working from eight in the morning to eight at night, and he would come home exhausted. He was constantly worn out. Neither of us have pensions, and we have to continue to make a living. But I was never worried because Stewart always has plans, and he is very pragmatic. He is also one of the most grounded human beings that I know. He knows he has to make some income, but he's so much happier working from home on projects he enjoys." Stewart agrees. "I am really enjoying living life rather than living my work," he said. "Now my goal is to get my wife semi-retired too. She is very stressed. Her work is extremely demanding. Clients expect more from her all the time and pay less and less. She also worries about her family. She has an aging parent and siblings with problems. Our challenge is to help her transfer to where I'm at. I know if we're both going to be semi-retired, we'll have to make some economies. But that won't be hard. We live very well now."

The supportive spouse can help her partner develop a post-retirement life by easing him into new activities. Harold's wife convinced him to join her club. "Harold is a big golfer and was never that interested in the stuff that went on at my social club. When he turned 70, I nudged him to join. He started out by going with me to the gym, and now he goes on his own as well. We have always liked to sing together in the car. So I convinced him we should join the choir. There are other things I have my eye on that I think might interest him, like the bridge club and the theatre outings, but I'm taking it a step at a time. He now knows more people at the club than I do." Since Harold's retirement, she's become the activity manager. "I've needed to become a more engaging companion. It's usually me who says in the morning, 'Here are the commitments in the day—where do we have some gaps? Here's an afternoon film we could see.' But in terms of trip planning he is the maestro and does a splendid job. So, in our relationship, we are both equal beings, both personally and profession- ally. And, although I'm as busy as I've ever been with my own work, I've re-organized things so that we can travel together more. I think the best quote about us is one that I think is from Kahlil Gibran: 'We have interconnection in our own solitude.'"

At age 73 Harold recently gave up several part-time work commitments and is happy to do things with his wife. "In my experience," he said, "those who have floundered in retirement are those who haven't been able to keep occupied. I was a widower when I married my second wife, and that was twelve years ago. We try and manage things so that we're both happy. She doesn't golf and I've been a keen golfer my whole life. We're going south for a few weeks next year. She doesn't like to drive there, and I don't like to leave her alone without a car. So I've made the decision that I won't bring my golf clubs. Otherwise I'd be leaving her stranded. So we're quite compatible. It's helpful we're still on our honeymoon. Some of my friends who have been together longer are finding it a bigger struggle."

Compromises

The relationships described above rely on both parties making compromises. As Caulfield's wife said, "We both give and get, or it doesn't work." But getting the balance right, so that both parties feel equally on the giving and receiving end, can be challenging. One of the reasons retirement requires compromises is that the retiree and his partner might not be on the same page in their dreams for the future. When TD Waterhouse surveyed Quebec retirees, they found that barely half of them had the same vision for retirement as their partners, and about one in five said there was conflict in their relationship because of their different retirement dreams.[9]

When both partners are still working flat-out, the issues requiring compromise may have yet to arise. At age 72 Patrick is still working full-time, and his wife is just as busy with a combination of work and volunteer commitments. "If she were in a different space," he said, "or if one of us were not as busy as the other, we would find ways as a couple to equalize this and figure out ways to do things together. But it works really well right now. We look for openings and take advantage of them to be together. It's fun to be just busy enough."

But when one of the partners has more time on his or her hands, compromises may be required. Ernest is 76 and, almost twenty years ago, retired from his full-time job. However, he replaced it almost immediately with a demanding volunteer position. "My wife and I are a bit out of sync. She doesn't like me being away, but I have chunks of time when I need to travel for my job, including an annual trip that's several weeks long. I can't give up the travel, but I try and reduce it by doing a lot on Skype. In the summer she wants me to be at the cottage for three months. When reliable Internet service wasn't available up there, this was a real problem. But since service has improved, I've been able to set up a good office. Now that I can work there, I'm fine with being at the cottage most of the summer. I'm an early riser, so I can get my work done in the morning, and that's working well. Often I'm finished my work before she even wakes up. On the other hand my wife loves adventurous travel and, if she could, she would have us travelling together to exotic places all the time. But, given my work commitments, this doesn't work for me."

Some people can minimize these kinds of conflicts by pursuing a joint dream. Andy and his wife are both in their late 60s and, over a decade ago, they retired from previous careers and moved to a small town to open a business. "We had been talking about doing this for years," Andy said. "It was New Year's Day 2001 that we resolved to either do something or stop talking about it. I wanted out of my job, but I needed to supplement my income. So one way or another there was going to be a career change. I had been an entrepreneur all my life, and I wasn't going to stop then. 'New' didn't scare either me or my wife." Andy's wife agrees. "I was ready for this adventure," she said, "but I didn't think Andy was. For my whole life I've been playing things by ear, and this move worked out even better than we expected. For one thing I thought this little town would be a cultural wasteland, but it's the opposite. There's a great symphony, and the theatre is going all the time."

Andy feels he and his wife have been successful at running a business together because they have different but complementary skills and interests. "My wife is more adept at some things," he said, "and I'm more adept at others. So working together works out just fine." They have no plans to retire. Andy's wife told me, "I can't imagine us ever stopping working. When we go on vacation, we get bored silly." Andy feels the same way. "As long as we're still excited to do this work," he said, "we'll be here. My motto is 'Don't retire, just change.' This way you avoid dealing with the disappointments that retirement can offer. It can be a crusher. What I think that could look like for me is falling off the cliff."

When spouses work together in their own company, there can be sufficient flexibility to develop a mutually agreeable retirement strategy. Lawson and his wife both work in his small business, and they have developed an approach to retirement that satisfies them both. "I'm 65 and have no intention of ever retiring, but my wife has convinced me to take more time off. So in the winter months, we spend two weeks a month in the south, and the rest of the year we work a three-and-a-half-day week. I've always been able to leave the office behind. So we're in sync about retirement. There's no conflict. We're soulmates."

Lawson's wife predicts her husband will never fully retire. "Lawson is very good at relaxing when we're down south, but I think it's because he knows he's going to work like a demon when he gets back. As far as his retirement goes, it's whatever he wants to do. As for me, when I feel I've had enough, I'll be comfortable retiring, whether he is still working or not. I really enjoy my job, but if I reach the point when I'm waking up and not wanting to go in to the office, then it's time to stop. When I retire, I'll be doing things that don't involve Lawson all the time. Right now we're glued to each other. He wants to do everything with me. I have a group of friends, but he doesn't. If he ever does retire, he's going to need stuff to do. If I can shoot him down the volunteer path, I think it will evolve on its own."

Real challenges can arise when the man is retiring at a time when his partner wants to ramp up her career. In cases where children have left home, the spouse may see the diminished demands of the empty nest as an opportunity to do something for herself. She may decide to seize the day and run for politics, take up art or writing, or go back to school. Following her passion will mean following her own schedule, and she may be spending less time at home just as her husband is spending more time there. If the man's goals don't mesh with her new life, cracks can emerge in the relationship, and men are taking different approaches to cementing the fissures. Some men tag along and hang out while their wives do their thing, and find fun in this approach. Others pursue their own interests and stay connected by scheduling those "we" times we talked about earlier.

Clayton falls into the latter category. As mentioned, after he retired his wife had an opportunity to put her career into full gear. So for the past five years, Clayton has been happily "keeping the house tidy and being a house husband." But this description he gives of himself diminishes the full life he's developed that includes much more then housework. "Being able to do a role reversal with my wife has been fun. The first year I did absolutely nothing but staying at home. I read, I relaxed, I gardened, I listened to music and I cooked. It was such a luxury. Now I do a day a week of consulting—just because the client approached me and the work is interesting. I figure I will continue this contract for at least another year or two, but I won't seek something else when it ends. I have never been bored in retirement. When people worry they will be bored, I say, 'Have you no personal interests? This is not possible.' Since I retired I've become a much better photographer and I've taken up piano. I swim a kilometre three times a week, cycle in summer, ski in winter, and walk around a nearby hiking trail whenever I can. There's always lots to do."

One of the reasons Clayton fell so easily into this role is that he's had practice. When their three children were very young, Clayton's wife went back to university. "She handed me the babies at night after I came home from work, and she went off to school." It also helped that Clayton was ready and willing to retire. "My last years were very tough and I was happy to leave when I did." Also, it helps that Clayton knows he and his wife will soon be spending more time together on their joint dream. "Every year since we were married, my wife and I have spent summer holidays in the community out East where she was born. Our goal is to spend more time there. For the last couple of years we have been planning it out. It's a moving target, but we'd like to live there from May to September. We have just finished building a fully insulated home, so we could even extend that to Thanksgiving."

In Clayton's case his wife was able to satisfy her ambitions with a job in the city where they live, and no relocation was required. But when the spouse's dream includes faraway places, life gets more challenging. I first encountered this dilemma several years ago when a friend I've known for decades came for a visit. He'd had the rug pulled out from under him and he wanted to talk. "My wife just announced that she wants to do her Ph.D.," he said. I was delighted to hear this and not altogether surprised. My friend's wife had put her academic career on hold while they were raising their family, and had taken a part-time job that allowed her to put the family first. Now the children were grown and off on their own adventures, and it seemed only fair for her to be off on one of her own. I didn't see the problem—until my friend added, "She wants to do her Ph.D. at Cambridge University." I knew he was ready to retire and had talked about returning to the kind of life he and his wife had pre-children—a time of joint adventures. He was taken aback to find out that his wife had a completely different vision for this next phase and one that was focused on fulfilling a dream of her own. "The Ph.D. program she wants to do," he added, "could take four to five years to complete." After the shock had worn off, my friend began to adjust to the new reality. He realized that his wife would only need to be in residence at the university for short periods, and while she was there, he could use Cambridge as a base for exploration. He had to admit it wasn't such a punishment to spend time in England with all of Europe at your doorstep. So he recalibrated his plans in a way that both supported his wife and gave him some new opportunities. But it was an adjustment.

Something similar happened to Bernard. He is 66 and in his seventh year of retirement, and he's spent a large portion of that time in South America supporting his wife's dream. "This adventure was conceived with a view to giving my wife an opportunity to teach at the university level," he explained. "She spent years at home when our children were young, and wallowed in less than stimulating jobs.

Then she got her Ph.D. and really wanted to put her degree to use. So she has the trump card in her hands, and I am along for the ride to make it happen." When Bernard first retired, he took a program of study that accredited him to teach English as a second language. This turned out to be a stroke of foresight. "My teaching skills have worked into a part-time job, and I like the appreciation I get from my students. I've realized that I need recognition. This is not easy to get when you've left not only your career but also your country. As well I don't have close male friends nearby, and I miss that." But, while it appears that Bernard is making a sacrifice for his wife, the reality is more nuanced. "My wife is frustrated at seeing my more relaxed lifestyle versus her working life. So there is certainly some envy. And she may need to delay retirement because of our financial circumstances. Although our children would like us to come home, we may need to continue on here for a while. As for me, overall, I'm enjoying retirement. I like not being bound by the expectations of too many others. And there's a benefit to living in South America at my age. I find there's more respect for seniors here than at home and less discrimination."

These stories illustrate the compromises that characterize relationships at this stage and highlight the importance of communication and trust. As Murray's wife said, "Communicating effectively is essential. And you've got to be honest with each other. Problems happen when one person is surreptitiously working on getting around the other person." She decided to kick-start her career at age 60, long after her husband had retired. "I love my work and would like to continue doing it as long as possible," she said. "But if Murray decided he wasn't happy living here and wanted to move someplace else, I would give it up." However, Murray seems happy with the status quo. "I see this process as a journey," he told me. "I'm keeping an ear open for my wife's plans and hope she'll keep working. It gives her such satisfaction. And even if she leaves this job, she'll probably move on to the next thing. I'm following the advice of our friend who said to me, 'This is clearly her dream, and you've got to get out of the way.'"

Sex after 60

At a time when a man is making major life adjustments and reworking his primary relationships, he is thrown an additional challenge—his sexuality is changing. The results can either improve his relationship with his partner or throw up additional barriers. Bruce didn't mince words about his sexual performance issues. "My erections don't come as often," he said. "For me that's a big disadvantage of getting older." Bruce is in his late 70s and retired a few years ago at age 75. He divorced his wife decades ago and has been living with his current partner for sixteen years. But while

Bruce's sexual performance may have diminished, his love for his partner is stronger than ever. "This relationship is the strength that is supporting my life today," he confided.

Barry and Emily McCarthy write in *Therapy with Men after Sixty* that the traditional male sex role that depends on perfect intercourse performance might work for men in their 20s and 30s, but it is self-defeating once men reach their 60s: "Men who cling to the traditional perfect intercourse performance usually stop being sexual in their fifties or sixties. They become trapped in the cycle of anticipatory anxiety, tense and failed intercourse performance, frustration, embarrassment, and eventually sexual avoidance." The McCarthys recommend that, instead of approaching intercourse as a pass-fail test, the man should view his partner as his intimate sexual friend with whom he shares pleasure rather than performs for. "With age, a great advantage is that couple sexuality becomes more intimate, creative, genuine, and interactive—the couple need each other to enhance sexual desire, function, and satisfaction."[10]

The McCarthys also debunk the stereotype that men are from Mars and women are from Venus when it comes to senior sex. While it is true that men and women in their teens and 20s approach sexual relationships and experience sexual response in different ways, with older men and women there are many more sexual similarities than differences. Like women, men want an intimacy that is about feeling securely attached and emotionally open to their partner.[11]

As mentioned previously, Caulfield is 65 and retired three years ago. He provides the textbook case for the McCarthys' description of the advantages of older sex. "Sex after 60 is really different," he told me, "because it's not about self-satisfaction or about getting off. It's about finding pleasure for both of you where you both receive and give. Your body is deteriorating, you can't get into the same positions, and you're much more cognizant of the other person. Being retired, I have more time available and I'm conscious of my wife's presence. I love hugging her and teasing her and touching her. I do think that women have a different libido, and for them it's less important. But I find that's not been the case for me. The feeling of another body close to yours is really important." Caulfield's wife sees sexuality as part of the adjustments the two of them are making at this stage of life. "The first couple of years of Caulfield's retirement were really difficult for him," she said, "so I really wanted to spend time supporting him. He was around a lot and thought we would spend all our time having sex. But I had things to do and places to go. We have never really been good at living in the house together, but we have always travelled well together. So, after we both got over the shock of not going into a job, we started to be together as though we were on a trip, and this is working well. We needed to figure it out."

Even the iconic ladies' man, singer and songwriter Leonard Cohen developed a new appreciation for his partners when he got older. "I never met a woman until I was sixty-five," Cohen admitted. Until then he had viewed women through his own "urgent needs and desires," and "what they could do for me." "Once that started to dissolve," he said, "I began to see the woman standing there." His biographer, Sylvie Simmons, writes in *I'm Your Man* that this period of his mid-60s was when the depression he had been battling started to lift. Cohen said that old age was the best thing that ever happened to him.[12]

Divorce

Turning to the third of the dreaded Ds, divorce, what are the odds of a marriage surviving the man's retirement? Provocative headlines tell us we're in the middle of a grey divorce revolution and report that "silver splitters" are at an all time high. Not surprisingly the facts are much more nuanced. The number of men divorcing when they are 65 and older is increasing slightly year over year, but the vast majority of marriages withstand the retirement years.[13] And longer marriages last longer. The highest number of divorces occur after the third or fourth anniversary, and the rate of divorce decreases for each additional year married.[14] However, divorce rates don't tell the whole story. Divorce rates in Canada have been declining over recent years.

One of the reasons is that more people are living common law. And common-law unions are growing fastest among people of retirement age.[15]

You read earlier about partnerships that were strengthened by the challenges of retirement. But too much togetherness can shine a spotlight on your partner's flaws. In *About Schmidt* the recently retired Warren Schmidt itemizes his dissatisfactions with his wife in a letter to Ndugu, a six-year-old boy from Tanzania, he has recently adopted through Child Reach. "Helen and I been married for forty-two years," he writes. "Lately every night I find myself asking the same question. Who is this old woman who lives in my house? Why is it that every little thing she does irritates me? Like the way she gets her keys out of her purse long before we reach the car. And how she throws our money away on her ridiculous little collections. And tossing out perfectly good food just because the expiry date is passed. And her obsession with trying new restaurants. And the way she cuts me off when I try to speak. And I hate the way she sits and the way she smells. For years now she has insisted that I sit when I urinate. My promise to lift the seat and wipe the ring and put the seat back down wasn't good enough for her."

If the film were to follow the stereotype, Schmidt would dump Helen and run off with a younger woman. While this situation does happen in real life, it is not the norm. Barry and Emily McCarthy report that, contrary to media myths about older marriages, it is the woman who decides to leave in over two in three cases, and the rates are even higher among college-educated couples. "The typical pattern is the woman is disappointed in the man and marriage," they write. "With children gone and no sign of relational improvement, her sense of disappointment and alienation grows, whether resulting in divorce or staying together in a distant manner."[16]

I heard several stories about post-retirement couples "staying together in a distant manner," as the McCarthys describe it. Once again the Japanese have an expression for this: *kateinai rikon*, or "in-family divorce."[17] Andy described such a situation. "I got to know a woman who was staying at the same B&B as my wife and me," he said. "She couldn't stand being at home with her husband, so after he retired she kept working. But eventually she had to retire. At that point she began making up excuses to travel. That was why she was a frequent guest at B&Bs."

Murray's wife has seen examples of "staying together in a distant manner" when there is a certain amount of bullying in a relationship. "In those cases," she said, "when the man moves back into the home full-time, the wife can't bear it. I know of a couple like that. He was an engineer and she was a nurse. They retired and moved to their cottage, which was really his dream. In the winter they lived virtually alone. As soon as she could, the wife got a job at the closest hospital even though it meant driving thirty-five miles every day. She couldn't get out of the house fast enough. She worked at the hospital for another ten years."

Lawson knows this story from the man's point of view. "I was meeting with my friend just this morning," he told me. "He runs his own business, and he really should retire. His memory is going and he knows it. His kids are leaning on me to try and get him to move along. But he says to me, 'What am I going to do if I retire? I can't stand my wife. I've been married for fifty years, and we can't bear to be in the same room together.'" Lawson goes on to explain that his friend's deteriorating work performance is hurting the business and is hard on the family. "Hopefully I'm going to be able to convince him that it's time to retire," he said.

The following joke, told to me by a retired man, seems to sum up situations like this one: "Why do men die sooner than their wives?" Answer: "They want to." And then there's this one: "Why are you getting divorced now at age 90?" Answer: "We were waiting for the children to die."

Sometimes people stay together because they can't afford not to. Victor and his wife are living together post-divorce for financial reasons, but they hope the situation is temporary. They both retired at the same time, and ending their foreign postings meant a return to Canada. "It was like a double divorce," Victor said. "We were leaving our jobs, as well as the place that had been our home for years.

When we moved back to Canada, we started off in a three-bedroom condo, and my wife really pushed me to buy a very expensive large house. It was a bad idea. Our relationship started to deteriorate almost right away. There was too much happening, too fast. We didn't have the chance to acclimatize. We moved into the house four years ago and divorced two years later. We've been trying to sell the house ever since and it's become an albatross. We couldn't afford to move out, so we divided up the living space. We lived under the same roof without speaking to one another for a year. But it became unbearable, so we took a trip together, and now it's a little better. Downsizing solo is next on the list—but first our house has to sell."

Barry and Emily McCarthy make the argument that men should work at marriage because married men live longer and healthier lives. And there is a significant body of research to support the McCarthys' conclusion that a satisfying, secure and sexual marriage is a major contributor to personal well-being for men after 60.[18] "That surprises, if not shocks, many men," they write. "Traditionally, men tended to take their marriages for granted and were unaware or unconcerned that the marital bond had atrophied." They say it is unwise for men to put their relationship on autopilot and settle for a marginal marriage. "The male should focus on revitalizing the marital bond for himself, not to placate his wife," they advise.[19]

As part of the Harvard Study of Adult Development, Dr. George Vaillant conducted a longitudinal study of hundreds of men over seven decades. The research concluded that for men, having a stable marriage, one without serious problems, is linked to aging successfully because it provides social, financial and emotional resources, and reduces stress.[20] Other research by Mary Elizabeth Hughes and Linda J. Waite looking at the link between marital biography and health found that people who have married once and remained married are consistently, strongly and broadly advantaged. Those who spent more years divorced or widowed have more chronic health conditions and mobility limitations. Among those who have ever been divorced or widowed, the remarried generally show better health than those who have remained unmarried, and those who spent more time married report fewer chronic conditions and mobility limitations."[21]

Certainly we're all better when we're loved, but men in particular seem to thrive in relationships. Research has found that they reported greater happiness when at home than at work, while, in contrast, women reported significantly greater happiness when at work than at home.[22] Men whose marriages end are at higher risk of depression than women. And breakups can reduce a man's social support network more than a woman's and impair his relationship with his children.[23]

In 2014 the UK International Longevity Centre released a report titled "Isolation: The emerging crisis for older men," which combined data from the "English longitudinal study of aging" with interviews, focus groups and research findings. The study found that overall older men reported less loneliness than older women. However, older men living alone were lonelier than women living alone. They found this to be the case because older men were dependent on their partners, and increasing numbers of older men were living alone.[24] At age 93 Roger Angell, the American essayist and editor for *The New Yorker*, wrote that the death of his wife had him yearning for "conversation and renewed domesticity." The biggest surprise of his life was to discover "our unceasing need for deep attachment and intimate love." "Everyone in the world," he writes, "wants to be with someone else tonight, together in the dark, with the sweet warmth of a hip or a foot or a bare expanse of shoulder within reach." If you've lost that, you never lose the longing to find it again, he says. "If it returns, we seize upon it avidly, stunned and altered again."[25]

This may seem like an argument for a man to be good to his partner and make the marriage work at all costs. As I like to tell my husband—"Happy wife, happy life." But a bad relationship causes both mental and physical damage, and, "if you can't fix a marriage, you're better off out of it." Those are the words of Janice Kiecolt-Glaser, an Ohio State scientist who studies the relationship between marital strife and immune response. In one study she measured the time it takes for a wound to heal and found that among couples who showed high levels of anxiety it took days longer for the healing process to take effect.[26] This was also the position of the elders I interviewed for my book *You Could Live a Long Time: Are You Ready?* They told me that staying in a bad relationship in your senior years is worse than going it alone.

Chris would agree. He has been an entrepreneur his whole life and finds himself at age 70 with not enough money and some serious health issues. "I didn't plan my retirement well," he said. "I have several projects that I work on, and from time to time I get income from them that supplements my pension. But I could use more money. And I'm worried about getting feeble. I have some depression that may be linked to an onset of Parkinson's. I'm part of a medical study that's looking into this. So you'd think I'd miss my marriage. But I don't. I was with my second wife for twenty-four years, and I'm much better off alone. I'm adaptable and good at being single. It's my first wife who looks out for me now. She has remarried and lives in another city, but she keeps in touch with me by phone and is always concerned about my welfare. And my three sons are my greatest strength."

When Chris says that the people supporting him are his ex-wife and his children, he reminds us that a man's emotional circle is not exclusively dependent on having a spouse.[27] My book *The Perfect Home for a Long Life* includes a wide variety of examples of older men who have structured their lives to create a supportive community. Dave used a home share service to locate a married couple with whom he could live. The homeowners, who are also seniors, welcomed Dave to live with them as a tenant, but treat him as part of their family. In another example, Alice and Judd, both 79 years of age, are former partners who split up in their 50s. Four years ago they moved back in together but this time both have their own floor. Alice finds lots of benefits in this "separate but together" arrangement. "It beats living together because it gives me a lot more choice over what I get to do," she said. "I can be with him or alone. I watch TV at his place and bring up my supper. If I need him in the middle of the night, he can get there quickly enough, and the same goes for me reaching him. I can call him if I have something heavy to lift."

Ned is 63 and rents out rooms to his friends in the heritage home he inherited from his mother. He is conscious that what they are creating in his house is about more than economics and obligations. "You have to have something spiritual to recognize you are a community," he explained. "So when we have an occasion to celebrate, we seize it. By celebrating, we have something we share, and people have something to feel a part of. We are battered veterans of life."

Statistics Canada found that seniors who report a strong sense of community belonging are more likely to be in good health than those who feel less connected.[28] And even if you're in poor health, you'll be less likely to suffer from depression if you have frequent contact with friends.[29] Dr. Michael Evans sees daily evidence of this in his medical practice. "Social isolation can be as powerful a risk factor as smoking," he says. "If I had a prescription for loneliness my day would be a lot easier."[30]

Terrance is 70 years of age and sees his father as a role model for creating community for himself. "My father was widowed in his late 70s," he said, "but that didn't slow him down. He began working part-time and also became an ardent artist. When he was 80, he was going out one afternoon, and I asked him what he was doing. He said he was going over to the Golden Age centre to teach some old people how to paint. That's where he met his 69-year-old blonde girlfriend, and he had three wonderful years with her before he died. "Watching my dad," he said, "I learned that as you age, you need a massive support system of spouse, friends, children, whomever. You never want to feel that you're alone physically or psychologically. You don't know what's coming, so you better have people that can help you through the tough times."

As for Warren and Helen's marriage in *About Schmidt*, we'll never know if their relationship could have survived his retirement. As the story goes, they weren't given the opportunity to try. While Schmidt is off mailing his letter to Ndugu, his wife drops dead in their kitchen of a blood clot in her brain. Going through her papers, Schmidt discovers that decades earlier Helen had an affair with Schmidt's best friend. He is furious, hurt and humiliated. But after a journey that includes sleeping under the stars on the top of his RV, he is able to see their relationship from her point of view. "I forgive you," he says. "That was a long time ago and I know I wasn't always the king of kings. I let you down. I'm sorry Helen. Can you forgive me?"

Relationship with Yourself

———◆———

Reaching retirement age can trigger questions about mortality and the meaning of life. For some of the men I interviewed, leaving the world of work precipitated a full-blown existential crisis, and they questioned their reason for being. For Darryl the emotional turmoil started when his projects were finished and he was well and truly retired. "What I didn't expect was the emotional hole at the end of my work," he said. "There is something at the heart of it that worries me. I'm afraid it's all meaningless. What does it matter? I did not expect this. It's been some time now, and I'm still searching. It makes me fearful, anxious. Right now I'm living that Peggy Lee song—'Is That All There Is?'"

Not everyone I interviewed felt their very foundation collapse to this degree, but all of them are doing some soul searching about their remaining years. Matthew Barrett, former CEO of the Bank of Montreal and then Barclays, Britain's largest bank, said he intended to put "care of the soul" on his retirement "to-do" list. When he was asked about his post-retirement plans he said, "It seems to me that you should divide your time three ways: into work, humanitarian pursuits, and sheer pleasure. I have a friend who's a psychiatrist, and she recommends putting care of the soul on that list. When you're trying to make your way, and you're scratching and clawing to get on in the world, you don't give much time or attention to the child within yourself. I think she'd advise us all to make that number four."[1]

Although the earlier discussions about *Death of a Salesman* and *About Schmidt* focused on retirement, these works are fundamentally about the hollowness of the American dream and the emptiness at the end of the "scratching and clawing to get on in the world," as Matthew Barrett puts it. My generation learned this lesson growing up in the '60s, and getting closer to the end of life is a big reminder of the limits of materialism and the slim support to be gained from the superficial.

An indictment of the values of consumerism and empty striving is a theme in Jack Kerouac's fictionalized autobiography *On the Road*, which was published in 1957 and came to be known as the testament of the Beat Generation. Several of the men I interviewed mentioned the influence of the Beat Generation on their thinking, referencing the writings of Jack Kerouac, Neal Cassady and Allen Ginsberg. The *Village Voice* reviewer called *On the Road* "a rallying

cry for the illusive spirit of rebellion of these times."[2] Bob
Dylan said he cherished it "like a Bible" in his youth.[3]

On the Road is a stream of consciousness narration of
several road trips across the country taken by two buddies,
the narrator, Sal Paradise (Jack Kerouac), and his friend,
Dean Moriarty (Neal Cassady.) The writer John Leland
describes the book as a primer for male friendship and "a
male fantasy that goes back to Huck and Tom or Jesus and
his disciples, who all chose starvation and travail over clean
laundry and the comforts of women. They are merry men
of misery, pushing each other to lives none can sustain."[4]

But Leland's book, *Why Kerouac Matters: The Lessons of On
the Road (They're Not What You Think)* persuaded me that
reading the book as merely an irresponsible male bonding
trip is missing the point. Kerouac saw the book's themes as
spiritual. "Dean and I were embarked on a tremendous journey through post-Whitman America to FIND that America
and to FIND the inherent goodness in American man. It was
really a story about 2 Catholic buddies roaming the country
in search of God. And we found him."[5] Leland reports that
On the Road contains twenty-three references to "kicks" but
as many to God or Jesus.[6] The Christian magazine *Touchstone*
said that the '60s had misinterpreted Kerouac's road as a
"fast lane of immediate gratification and mindless pleasure"
when it should be seen as "the ultimate test of both physical
and spiritual endurance." "He [Sal/Kerouac] wants to find

in America a strange new world that defies the materialism and conformity of the fifties."[7]

Reading *On the Road*, I was struck by the way the following passage echoes Matthew Barrett's description of "scratching and clawing to get on in the world." Sal says, "I had traveled eight thousand miles around the American continent and I was back on Times Square; and right in the middle of rush hour, too, seeing with my innocent road-eyes the absolute madness and fantastic hoorair of New York with its millions and millions hustling forever for a buck among themselves, the mad dream—grabbing, taking, giving, sighing, dying, just so they could be buried in those awful cemetery cities beyond Long Island City."[8]

When I interviewed Ralph, he told me the Beat Generation had always appealed to him, especially the concept of the road trip. "The men of the Beat Generation were a bit directionless," he said, "but enjoying everything about every day. I love the idea of a road trip. I did one by myself, 'just enjoying everything about every day,' visiting Walden Pond and Emerson's house. Another great trip I took in the same vein was going to Mississippi and Tennessee for music, including Graceland." Although the road trip connection with the Beat Generation was top of mind for Ralph, his attitude towards his work also reflects their messages about fighting materialism and conformity. "Work has always been a means to an end for me," Ralph said. "I don't care what other men think of me really. They measure their lives completely differently from me. My car is seven years old, and I am not interested in buying a new one because I use it so rarely. I cycle everywhere. So I don't care about having the latest car."

The men I interviewed are seeking spiritual connection in a myriad of ways, both structured and unstructured. As the Persian poet Rumi wrote, care of one's soul can take many forms. "There are hundreds of ways to kneel and kiss the ground." Some participate in organized religion, some have personal belief practices, some nourish their soul by giving to others and their community. Many of the men I interviewed see retirement as an opportunity to spend more time on these endeavours.

Terrance is using photography to explore spirituality, Chris has taken up painting to understand what shapes represent, and Terry is trying to figure out the meaning of life and our role in the universe. Caulfield is separating from things and focusing more strongly on an inner life. "Acquiring things is not part of this phase," he said. "This is a transference phase, so I'm giving things away. I am reading poetry. It's a lot of self-examination. It's painful and it's difficult. But I'm really wanting to look at things that I haven't put to rest. I feel I haven't yet extracted their meaning. Like R. D. Laing says, 'Don't be reluctant to go through things.'"

Leonard Cohen chose to focus his exploration on Buddhism. As previously described, when Cohen was approaching his 60th birthday he decided to move to a monastery to live in a small bare hut on a mountain to learn from his 90-year-old Buddhist teacher. Cohen had been finding it difficult to write authentically and felt the problem might have to do with a sense of mortality, "that this whole enterprise is limited, that there was an end in sight."[9] He was drawn to the monastery by "the sense of something unfinished, something that would keep me alive."[10] Three years into his life in the monastery, he was ordained a Zen Buddhist monk.

According to Statistics Canada, well over half of seniors aged 75 and over say that spiritual beliefs are very important in the way they live their lives, and about half of them attend religious services at least once a month. They say that these beliefs help them to understand life's difficulties and find meaning in their lives.[11] Research from the United Kingdom has confirmed this link between emotional well-being and religious beliefs in older people, and some of the benefits may well spring as much from the value of belonging to a group as from the belief system per se. Researchers found that religious beliefs provide older people with a sense of purpose, and offer participation in a supportive social network. Actively participating in religious events can bring even greater benefits.[12]

Recent research found that religiosity both protected older adults against depression and helped individuals recover from depression. Both organizational and non-organizational forms of religiosity were effective in different circumstances. Older adults who were not depressed at the study's inception remained non-depressed two years later if they frequently attended religious services. Those who were depressed were less likely to be depressed at follow-up if they more frequently engaged in private prayer. The researchers recommended improving access and transportation to places of worship for those interested in attending services as well as facilitating discussions about religious activities and beliefs with clinicians.[13]

When I interviewed the elders for *You Could Live a Long Time: Are You Ready?* they emphasized the importance of having values and moral beliefs to guide and sustain them as they aged. "Without a moral compass, you get buffeted around," one man said. In some cases their belief systems were expressed through organized religion; in other cases they led secular lives that were grounded in a sense of morality and purpose. Georgina said, "You need some form of belief system as you age. I haven't become more devoted as I age. I actually find I have more questions, rather than less. But my religion really grounds me. It's the center of my outlook and it guides me." Some of the elders used techniques such as yoga, journaling, visualization and guided imagery, and working with the breath. Techniques such as these are part of a wide range of activities that have been shown to replenish physical, emotional and spiritual energy.[14]

One very effective way to care for your soul is to give to others. This is one of the lessons taught by Confucius: "I sought for happiness and happiness eluded me; I turned to service and happiness found me." Most of the men I interviewed were contributing to their communities in ways that ranged from working in soup kitchens to serving on non-profit boards, from mentoring the next generation to running volunteer organizations. Many of them view retirement as an opportunity to spend more time in civic engagement.

Jean Vanier, the Catholic philosopher, theologian and humanitarian who founded l'Arche, an international organization of communities for the developmentally disabled, says we need to break out of the shell of self-centredness if we are to mature. In *Becoming Human* Vanier reminds us that any effort we make to connect with others, no matter how small, is valuable. "But let us not put our sights too high. We do not have to be saviours of the world! We are simply human beings, enfolded in weakness and in hope, called together to change our world one heart at a time."[15]

It turns out that volunteering with children is a particularly effective way to nourish one's soul. Experience Corps works in cities throughout the United States providing volunteers over the age of 55 as tutors and mentors to elementary school children. At the same time that the program boosts student academic performance and helps schools become more successful, it also enhances the well-being of the volunteers. Seniors who volunteered with the program showed increased levels of physical, cognitive and social activity. Researchers concluded that for older people, when a cognitive activity is embedded in a generative activity (volunteering, civic organizations, assisting others), it makes the activity more personally enriching. People place more value on the activity beyond the immediate personal benefit and sustain their interest longer— which contributes to successful aging.[16] Another study that looked at an intergenerational project involving a preschool and a retirement community found that the seniors' spirituality was enhanced by the experience. They gained a sense of relatedness to others and a hope for the future.[17]

When author Daniel Klein was in his 70s, he went to Greece to see whether the philosopher Epicurus could teach him about the pleasures available only late in life. Epicurus saw the emptiness in striving as the hallmark of men in their prime, and believed that old age was the pinnacle of life. "It is not the young man who should be considered fortunate but the old man who has lived well, because the young man in his prime wanders much by chance, vacillating in his beliefs, while the old man has docked in the harbor, having safeguarded his true happiness."[18] In *Travels with Epicurus,* Klein says it would be a mistake to take the preoccupations of one's prime into old age because there is no rest for the striver. As soon as one goal on the "bucket list" is completed, another looms ahead. "And we have no time left for a calm and reflective appreciation of our twilight years, no deliciously long afternoons sitting with friends or listening to music or musing about the story of our lives. And we will never get another chance for that."[19]

Denis Healey, the retired British Labour politician who was a member of Parliament for over forty years, is relishing old age. "Psychologically I have widened," he said. "I have lost all my interest in power and position and no longer worry about making money. I am much more interested in people as human beings and can imagine them at every age from childhood onwards when I see them. . . . I am now much more sensitive to colours, shapes and sounds. . . . I enjoy music even more than I used to because I get greater pleasure out of the sound of different instruments. . . . I love my wife, my children and grandchildren more than ever and have much more time with them. To use Freud's expression, I have lost interest in my ego, much preferring my superego, while my id continues to wane."[20]

Conclusion

When I began my research into men and retirement, I worried it would be a depressing journey—and not just because of the infamous four Ds. I started feeling down about retirement after reading *Something to Live For: Finding Your Way in the Second Half of Life*, one of the books recommended by retirement counsellors. Written by coaches and educators Richard Leider and David Shapiro, the book weaves retirement advice through an account of a journey the two men took with some dozen other men in northern Tanzania. The purpose of the journey was to gain wisdom from the lives of the people they encountered that could be applied to the second half of their lives. The book is admirable in many respects, but I found its operating premise to be profoundly discouraging. The course of a man's life is described as follows: "We 'climb the ladder of success' in our careers; we rise 'from the outpost to the penthouse;' if we're lucky and work hard we'll ascend to 'the top of the heap.'" From that point on, Leider and Shapiro say life is a downhill slide. One of their goals in writing their book was "to explore that descending path." They ask the question, "What can we do to make the downward arc of our life's time and energy as rewarding and exciting as things were on the way up?"[1] They not only see the slide as inevitable, they also see it as lonely. "Descending, you're pretty much on your own. Each of us has to find his or her own way. And because of this, it's much harder to get the kind of support that enabled us to ascend so easily in the first place."[2]

I wondered if this truly was the way men saw their life trajectory—as peaking at the top of their careers, followed by a sharp and lonely decline. If they have such a debilitating personal vision, retirement must be a terrifying prospect. So I asked the men I interviewed to put pen to paper and draw me a visual representation of their life path. I even weighted the outcome towards a Leider and Shapiro representation by phrasing the question, "Draw your life path on a piece of paper and place yourself on it at this moment in time." People took my request very seriously, and even those who said they found the assignment difficult were able to come up with an image. I am heartened to report that not a single person drew his life as a downhill slide.

Some men positioned themselves on a simple line with estimates of how old they would be when their life would end. Hal said he would draw his life as a straight line with 70 two-thirds of the way along and 100 at the end point. "It's a constant progression," he said. "I'm not in decline. I have a whole range of things I've got to do, including four places in the world I want to see. But my life work is that I'm desperate to make my wife laugh."

Willis sees his life as a series of mountains and valleys that continue to project out in time. "I don't see a gentle decline," he told me. "The peaks are when I am thoroughly engaged. I like the intellectual development and intensity of engagement in a given subject area. And then I enjoy linking it to action." His wife imagined that he would draw his life as many forks in the road with long tongs between the forks. "And along each road there would be parallels to other experiences he's had," she said. "He's been able to build on what he's learned at all these moments of experience. And he's done this all without acquiring a lot of barnacles. He remains 'uncynical.'"

Ralph drew two different visual representations of his life. One showed it as ascending on a graph with time on the bottom and satisfaction on the vertical. The other was a pie chart with the wedges representing the percentage of the things in his life that were under his control. "I like to have the pie all green and all happy, meaning I'm doing things I find satisfying," he said.

Ryan sees his life course as multiple strands that intersect. "The strands are work, family, relationships, health, and they all interplay," he explained. "They're not highs and lows. They move in and out along a timeline. It's like a sound metre with the lines vibrating at different levels of intensity."

Caulfield drew an image of a series of concentric forms subsiding and expanding. "These are bubbles descending and surfacing and coming up for air," he said. "It's a dance. Sometimes we get dizzy and sometimes we have different partners, but ultimately it's revolving around itself. It's a savouring and a masticating and a revisiting of your memories and trying to feed yourself with what it means."

Parry sees his life path as a process of understanding himself and the human condition. "I don't perceive my life as a linear pattern," he told me. "It is multi-dimensional. It's a transformation and a distilling—a transmogrification. It is a becoming rather than a path. It's a search pattern with continuity. It's a process of clarifying who you are as a human being and seeing through the social trappings.

For Andy his life course is a series of spirals or circles around the path—the path being determined by his comfort level. "If it disappears, then I have to start rethinking my life course," he said. Murray sees his life as chapters in his life's book. Gerry sees his life as riding a series of waves. Gene says his lifeline is like a prairie road stretching out in front of him. "I have so many things I want to do, and I'm so far behind I'll never complete them in the years I have left," he confessed.

These eloquent descriptions are an affirmation that retirement for the men I interviewed will be a continuation of the lives they have been leading, lives of great variety and endless possibility. Retirement is allowing them to compose new movements in their lives' musical scores.

Now that we have put to rest the notion that retirement is necessarily a time of decline, and minimized the impact of the four dreaded Ds, I propose we replace the Ds with more accurate descriptors. I'm suggesting some Cs—continuity, challenge, choice, creativity and capacity.

When I interviewed Ernest, he told me a story that illustrates the Cs in action. I had asked Ernest whether he had a role model for his retirement and he named Harry, the hired hand who had been working on their farm for decades. He described the following incident to illustrate why his goal in retirement is to emulate Harry. "One day my father and his two brothers, all of whom were well into their 70s, were working on shoring up a piece of the barn that was falling down," Ernest recounted. "Harry was 90 years old at the time, and although he was officially retired, he still liked helping out. For all these men, work was fun. I was 10 years old, just hanging around watching them. They needed to put a huge beam in place and decided to put if off until the following Saturday when they'd come back to the farm with the equipment they needed, and my dad and uncles would put the beam up. The beam must have weighed 600 to 700 pounds. When they came back the next Saturday, they found the beam was already in place. Harry had done it all by himself using a car jack. I was amazed. To me Harry always seemed so frail a strong wind could have knocked him down. Yet he had accomplished what was going to take these three men using a motorized tool to do. Harry had a job to do, he had a week to do it in, and he was going to get it done."

Ernest's story encapsulates the Cs of retirement. Retirement is neither a dramatic departure from the course nor a slip down the slope, rather it is another step along the *continuity* of one's life. There will be *challenges* and *choices*, but men have a wellspring of *creativity* and *capacity* to draw on, resources they have developed over a lifetime.

There's another C word I'd like to propose and that's *compassion*. I said at the beginning I wasn't going to tell men what to do, but I do have a suggestion. As you're negotiating retirement, try not to be too hard on yourself. Many of the men I interviewed talked about "letting themselves down" or "being disappointed in themselves" because they weren't adjusting quickly enough to retirement, or hadn't anticipated some outcome, or for any number of reasons. Albert's wife is finding that in retirement he has the same anxiety he had in his work day. "He approaches retirement with absolute intensity," she said. "I'd like him to realize when things are not the most important in the world. His drive is still alive and kicking, and I wish he'd settle down a bit and chill out. I have to give him permission to calm down."

Darryl is finding this about himself as well. "I have a very high standard for myself, and I rarely meet it," he confessed. "My wife says I must learn to forgive myself. I don't know why I'm this way. It blindsides me from time to time. I don't have a role model, but here's my ideal person. He would be more serene in his view of the world, less judgmental of himself, more accepting of his own faults and joyful about the future."

To ease up on themselves and find their equanimity, some of the men I interviewed are drawing on the messages of their youth in the '60s—mantras that emphasize the journey over the destination, going with the flow and the importance of living consciously. Caulfield says his role model for retirement is an 85-year-old man who was his former teacher. "He has really developed as a human being," Caulfield told me. "He takes pleasure in crunching into a fresh picked apple, or having a great conversation with a young person he's just met, or savouring a very old piece of cheese a vendor gave him at the market. He wants to experience it all. I consider him a bodhisattva, a wise being."

And this brings me to a final additional C word—*child-like*. When I interviewed Terry and asked him about the happiness he has found in retirement, he talked about becoming more deeply engaged in life's little pleasures.

"As I get older, I find I'm getting the same sense of enjoyment in small things that I had as a kid," he said. "Zorba the Greek is my role model for retirement." Several of the men I interviewed talked about Zorba as their role model because of the way he embraces life at his advanced age. Nikos Kazantzakis wrote the book *Zorba the Greek,* and here is his description of the joyful man of fierce appetites that he created. "Like the child, [Zorba] sees everything for the first time. He is for ever astonished and wonders why and wherefore. Everything seems miraculous to him, and each morning when he opens his eyes he sees trees, sea, stones and birds, and is amazed."[3] Sounds like the description of a good retirement.

Acknowledgements

———•◦•◦•———

This book was built on the foundation of the lives of sixty-one people—forty-four men and seventeen of their partners—who told me their stories about being (or living with) a retirement-aged man. Because they spoke with great candour about themselves, their workplaces and their families, I have changed their names and disguised identifying characteristics. I am profoundly grateful for the trust they placed in me. The honesty with which they described their lives has provided a deep well of experience on which the reader can draw.

I would also like to thank the reviewers who gave me thoughtful feedback on an early draft of the book. They are Tim Christian, Eric and Dorothy Dahli, Kaija and Dick Dickson, Vince Gilpin, Bill Graham, Hank Intven, Helen McDonald, Lawrence Pillon, Suzanne Robinson and Dr. Samir Sinha. The book has benefited greatly from their insights and knowledge.

Ready to Retire? owes its existence to my editor, Patrick Crean, who brings character and integrity to an unerring ability to identify the issues that matter. It's a dream to be supported by the excellence of the HarperCollins team.

A special thanks goes to Hank, Lauren, Andrea, Diego and Zach, who inspire me daily.

Endnotes

Men and Retirement

1 According to the Statistics Canada 2011 census, there are a total of 1,002,685 men aged 60 to 64. There are an additional 738,010 men aged 65 to 69. http://www12.statcan.gc.ca/census-recensement/2011/dp-pd/prof/index.cfm?Lang=E.

2 Gail Sheehy, *Understanding Men's Passages: Discovering the New Map of Men's Lives* (New York: Random House, 1998), p. 4.

3 Ibid., p. 5.

4 See, for example, Raymond Bossé, Carolyn M. Aldwin, Michael R. Levenson and Kathryn Workman-Daniels, "How stressful is retirement? Findings from the normative aging study," *Journal of Gerontology: Psychological Sciences* 46, no. 1 (1991): 9–14.

5 Sheehy, *Understanding Men's Passages*, p. 7.

6 For more on the power of the unconscious mind, see Leonard Mlodinow, *Subliminal: How Your Unconscious Mind Rules Your Behavior* (New York: Vintage Books, 2013).

Fears of Retirement

1 Talcott Parsons and Robert Freed Bales, *Family: Socialization and Interaction Process* (Glencoe, IL: Free Press, 1955), p. 22.

2 Sheehy, *Understanding Men's Passages*, p. 18.

3 These quotations are from the Penguin Plays (New York: 1976) edition of Arthur Miller's *Death of a Salesman: Certain Private Conversations in Two Acts and a Requiem*, first published 1949.

4   Charles Isherwood, *"A play that resounds in the heart and the gut,"* *New York Times*, April 20, 2012.
5   The director writing in the DVD extras.
6   Quoted in Alain de Botton, *Status Anxiety* (Toronto: Penguin Canada, 2004), p. 8.
7   Franz Kafka, *The Trial* (New York: Random House, 1995), p. 20.
8   John Updike, *Rabbit at Rest* (New York: Random House, 1990), pp. 84, 82.

The Reality of Retirement

1   Statistics Canada CANSIM Table 282-0209.
2   Rob Pascal, Louis H. Primavera and Rip Roach, *The Retirement Maze* (Lanham, MD: Rowan & Littlefield, 2012).
3   Paul B. Baltes and Peter Graf, "Psychological aspects of aging: facts and frontiers," in *The Lifespan Development of Individuals*, ed. David Magnusson (Cambridge: Cambridge University Press, 1996), p. 449.
4   Cited in J. R. Nininger, *The Public Service in Transition* (Ottawa: Canadian Centre for Management Development, 2003).
5   Pascal et al., *The Retirement Maze*, p. 144.
6   W. Somerset Maugham, *A Writer's Notebook* (New York: Vintage International, 2009), p. 332.
7   Dr. Gene Cohen, *The Mature Mind: The Positive Power of the Aging Brain* (New York: Basic Books, 2005), p. 151.
8   George E. Vaillant, M.D., *Aging Well* (New York: Little, Brown and Company, 2002), p. 48. Vaillant builds on the work of Erik Erikson, the psychoanalyst who developed eight stages of development.
9   Pascal et al., *The Retirement Maze*, p. 196.
10 S. LaRochelle-Côté, J. Myles and G. Picot. 2010. *Replacing family income during the retirement years: How are Canadians doing?* Statistics Canada Catalogue no. 11F0019M. Ottawa, Ontario. Analytical Studies Branch Research Paper Series, no. 328.
11 McKinsey & Company, *Building on Canada's Strong Retirement Readiness*, 2015.

12 *Sun Life Canadian Unretirement Index Report 2015*, Sun Life Financial, http://www.sunlife.ca/Canada/sunlifeCA/About+us/Canadian+Unretirement+Index?vgnLocale=en_CA.

13 Jonathan Chevreau, "Old enough to know better," *Financial Post*, January 26, 2012.

14 McKinsey & Company, *Building on Canada's Strong Retirement Readiness*, 2015.

15 Heavy drinkers were defined as those men who consume five or more alcoholic drinks on one occasion at least once per month. J. Park, 2010. *Health factors and early retirement among older workers.* Statistics Canada Catalogue no. 75-001-X. Ottawa, Ontario. Perspectives on Labour and Income.

16 There have also been attempts to argue that those who retire early live longer, but the research that makes that claim has also been debunked. See, for example, Richard Knight and Charlotte McDonald, "Do those who retire early live longer?" *BBC News Magazine*, July 23, 2012, http://www.bbc.com/news/magazine-18952037.

17 *The Chief Public Health Officer's Report on the State of Public Health in Canada, 2010.*

18 Heavy drinking is defined as having five drinks or more on a single occasion for men, and four or more drinks on a single occasion for women. E. M. Adlaf, P. Begin and E. Sawka (eds.), *Canadian Addiction Survey (CAS): A national survey of Canadians' use of alcohol and other drugs: Prevalence of use and related harms: Detailed report.* Ottawa: Canadian Centre on Substance Abuse, 2005.

19 Freeman and Freeman, *The Stressed Sex* (Oxford: Oxford University Press, 2013), p. 147.

20 "10 Myths and Realities About Aging," presentation by Dr. Samir Sinha, Director of Geriatrics at Mount Sinai Hospital, http://www.mountsinai.on.ca/about_us/news/2013-news/mount-sinai2019s-dr-samir-sinha-shares-10-myths-and-realities-about-aging.

21 *The Chief Public Health Officer's Report on the State of Public Health in Canada, 2010.*

22 This research was restricted to studies of those under 65 years of age. Freeman and Freeman, *The Stressed Sex*, p. 113.

23 Edgar M. Bronfman and Catherine Whitney, *The Third Act: Reinventing Yourself After Retirement* (New York: Putnam, 2002), p. 111.

24 Ernest Hemingway, *The Old Man and the Sea* (New York: Scribner, 1952), p. 11.

25 Ibid., p. 23.

26 Albert J. DeFazio III, ed. *Dear Papa, Dear Hotch: The Correspondence of Ernest Hemingway and A. E. Hotchner* (Columbia, MS: University of Missouri Press, 2005), p. xvii.

27 Atul Gawande, *Being Mortal* (Toronto: Doubleday Canada, 2014), p. 95.

28 Daniel Klein, *Travels with Epicurus* (New York: Penguin Books, 2012), p. 5.

29 Gawande, *Being Mortal*, p. 27.

30 Ibid., p. 33.

31 Sharon-Dale Stone, "Age-Related Disability" in *The Ages of Life: Living and Aging in Conflict?* Ulla Kriebernegg, Roberta Maierhofer, eds. *Aging Studies* 3 (2013) Verlag, Bielefeld, pp. 66–67.

32 Leo Damrosch, *Jonathan Swift: His Life and His World* (New Haven: Yale University Press, 2013), p. 266.

33 Ibid., p. 464.

34 Ibid., p. 467.

35 McCarthy and McCarthy, *Therapy with Men after Sixty* (New York: Routledge, 2015), p. 78.

36 Ibid., p. 147.

37 Neil Strauss, *Everyone Loves You When You're Dead: Journeys into Fame and Madness* (New York: HarperCollins, 2011), p. 51.

38 Bronfman, *The Third Act*, p. 110.

39 For research from the frontiers of neuroplasticity, see Norman Doidge's books *The Brain That Changes Itself* (New York: Viking, 2007) and *The Brain's Way of Healing* (New York: Viking, 2015).

40 "10 Myths and Realities About Aging," http://www.mountsinai. on.ca/about_us/news/2013-news/mount-sinai2019s-dr-samir-sinha-shares-10-myths-and-realities-about-aging.

41   G. W. Rebok, K. Ball, T. Lin, R. N. Guey, H-Y. K. Jones et al., "Ten-year effects of the advanced cognitive training for independent and vital elderly cognitive training trial on cognition and everyday functioning in older adults," *Journal of the American Geriatrics Society* 62, no. 1 (January 2014): 16–24.

42   Anne Trafton, MIT News Office, "The rise and fall of cognitive skills: Neuroscientists find that different parts of the brain work best at different ages," March 6, 2015, http://newsoffice.mit.edu/2015/brain-peaks-at-different-ages-0306.

43   This research was cited in Daniel Klein, *Travels with Epicurus*, p. 71.

44   "Change Your Mindset, Change the Game," TEDx talk given by Dr. Alia Crum, a professor of psychology at Stanford University. Published on June 18, 2014, http://tedxtalks.ted.com/video/Change-Your-Mindset-Change-the.

45   Becca Levy and Ellen Langer, "Aging free from negative stereotypes: Successful memory in China among the American deaf," *Journal of Personality and Social Psychology* 66, no. 6 (June 1994): 989–997.

46   Becca R. Levy, "Mind matters: Cognitive and physical effects of aging self-stereotypes," *Journal of Gerontology: Psychological Sciences* 58B, no. 4 (2003): 203–211.

47   T. M. Hess, J. T. Hinson, E. A. Hodges, "Moderators of and mechanisms underlying stereotype threat effects on older adults' memory performance," *Experimental Aging Research* 35, no. 2 (2009): 153–177.

48   Images of Rembrandt's self-portraits can be found at the Web Museum at www.Ibiblio.org.

49   Roger Housden, *How Rembrandt Reveals Your Beautiful, Imperfect Self* (New York: Random House, 2005), p. 10.

50   Pascal et al., *The Retirement Maze*, p. 56.

51   Esi Edugyan, *The Second Life of Samuel Tyne: A Novel* (Toronto: Vintage Canada, 2005), p. 306.

52   "Ben Heppner, star tenor, announces retirement from singing," CBC News, April 24, 2014.

53   Pascal et al., *The Retirement Maze*, p. 56.

54 Gene D. Cohen, *The Mature Mind: The Positive Power of the Aging Brain* (New York: Basic Books, 2005), p. 144.

55 *The Next Chapter*, December 15, 2014, http://www.cbc.ca/ player/RADIO+HOLDING+PEN/Masseys/ID/2635629513/.

Delayed Retirement

1 As an indication of the diminishing importance of employment income as we age, by age 75, employment income accounts for less than 10 per cent of total income. *National Household Survey, 2011.* Statistics Canada Catalogue no. 99-014-X2011001. Ottawa, Ontario.

2 Statistics Canada CANSIM Table 282-0209. D. Duchesne, 2004. *More Seniors at Work.* Statistics Canada Catalogue no. 75-001-XIE. Ottawa, Ontario. Perspectives on Labour and Income.

3 *Sun Life Canadian Unretirement Index Report 2015*, Sun Life Financial, http://www.sunlife.ca/Canada/sunlifeCA/About+us/ Canadian+Unretirement+Index?vgnLocale=en_CA.

4 In 2006, seniors who turned 65 could expect to live nearly 20 additional years, 18 years for men and 21 years for women. *The Chief Public Health Officer's Report on the State of Public Health in Canada, 2010.*

5 For a good overview of the mandatory retirement debate, see Thomas R. Klasses, *Retirement in Canada* (Toronto: Oxford University Press, 2013).

6 J. Erfurt, A. Peppes and M. Purdy, *The Seven Myths of Population Aging: How Companies and Governments Can Turn the "Silver Economy" into an Advantage*, Accenture, 2012, https://ec.europa. eu/research/innovation-union/pdf/active-healthy-ageing/ accenture.pdf. See also E. Cox, G. Henderson and R. Baker, *Silver Cities: Realizing the Potential of Our Growing Older Population* (IPPR North, Manchester: 2014).

7 Christopher Loch et al., "The globe: How BMW is defusing the demographic time bomb," *Harvard Business Review*, March 2010.

8 Michael Skapinker, "Opinion: 'Age is your company's problem'" *Financial Times*, April 21, 2015.

9   Sodexo news release, "Sodexo receives 2014 best employers award for 50 plus Canadians," April 22, 2014, http://ca.sodexo.com/caen/ media/news-releases/140422-best-50-plus-employers-award.aspx.

10   In 2006, 44 per cent of senior men who had a job were self-employed. In 2014, the average retirement age was 63, whereas it was 66.4 for those self-employed. Statistics Canada CANSIM Table 282-0051. S. Uppal, 2011. *Seniors' self-employment.* Statistics Canada Catalogue no. 75-001-X. Ottawa, Ontario. Perspectives on Labour and Income.

11   For a discussion of the pros and cons of the on-demand economy see "There's an app for that," *Economist,* January 3, 2015, pp. 17–20.

12   Kerry Hannon, "For many older Americans, an enterprising path," *New York Times,* February 7, 2014.

13   See http://www.ctrpl.org/entrepreneurship-success-stories.

14   S. H. Patel and C. Grey, "Grey entrepreneurs in the UK," IKO working paper no. 18. Open University Research Centre on Innovation, Knowledge and Development, 2006.

15   Ibid., 12.

16   As well, significant numbers say they returned to take advantage of an interesting work opportunity or because they did not like retirement. Other reasons include wanting a challenge, wanting to make a contribution, preferring gradual retirement, an improvement in health and their caregiving duties no longer being required. J. Park. 2011. *Retirement, health and employment among those 55 plus.* Statistics Canada Catalogue no. 75-001-X. Ottawa, Ontario. Perspectives on Labour and Income.

17   Tavia Grant, "Freedom 68?" *Globe and Mail,* March 9, 2011.

18   Jeanne Beker, "Music doesn't impress me, fashion doesn't impress me," *Globe and Mail,* February 28, 2015.

19   Andy Greene, "After 15 years, Leonard Cohen proves he's still got it in Toronto," *Rolling Stone,* June 9, 2008, http://www.rollingstone. com/music/news/after-15-years-leonard-cohen-proves-hes-still-got-it-in-toronto-20080609.

20   Sylvie Simmons, *I'm Your Man: The Life of Leonard Cohen* (Toronto: McClelland & Stewart, 2012), p. 512.

21   Ibid., p. 527.

22   Claire Tomalin, *Charles Dickens: A Life* (London: Penguin, 2011), p. 354.

Relationships with Others

1   Seventy-nine per cent of men aged 65 to 74 are part of a couple, whether married or common-law. A. Milan, 2013. *Marital Status: Overview, 2011* Statistics Canada Catalogue no. 91-209-X. Ottawa, Ontario. Report on the Demographic Situation in Canada.

2   Michael Adams with Amy Langstaff, *Stayin' Alive: How Canadian Baby Boomers Will Work, Play, and Find Meaning in the Second Half of Their Adult Lives* (Toronto: Viking Canada, 2010), p. 63.

3   I use the term "wife" or "spouse" to refer to both married and unmarried partners. It is not intended to convey the legal status of the relationship.

4   "The New Lifestyles of Japanese Women," a speech by Sumiko Iwao, delivered in Lima, Peru, 1996, http://www.mofa.go.jp/j_info/japan/opinion/iwao.html.

5   Sheridan Prasso, *The Asian Mystique* (New York: Public Affairs, 2006), p. 175.

6   Anthony Failoa, "Sick of their husbands in graying Japan," *Washington Post*, October 17, 2005.

7   Pascal et al., *The Retirement Maze*, pp.158–159.

8   As an example, the 2005 Statistics Canada survey found that women aged 25 to 54 averaged almost two hours more per day on unpaid work activities than their male counterparts, time spent mainly on cooking, cleaning and household chores. C. Lindsay, 2008. *Are women spending more time on unpaid domestic work than men in Canada?*, 2008. Component of Statistics Canada Catalogue no. 89-630-X. Ottawa, Ontario. Matter of Fact Series.

9   "Does retirement make the heart grow fonder? TD Waterhouse surveys retired couples to find out," TD news release, February 18, 2010, http://td.mediaroom.com/index.php?s=19518&item=35846.

10   Barry McCarthy and Emily McCarthy, *Therapy with Men after Sixty*, p. 15.

11 Ibid., p. 57.

12 Simmons, *I'm Your Man* (p. 460) is quoting from an interview by Christine Langlois, CARP, June 2006.

13 Statistics Canada reported in 2008 there were 2,486 divorces among men 65 years of age and older. In 2005 the number was 2,291. To put this in context, in 2008 there were 1,410,855 men aged 65 years and over who were married. Statistics Canada discontinued collection of marriage and divorce data after 2008.

14 Using Statistics Canada data, Dr. Ambert reports that the highest number of divorces occurs after the third and fourth anniversaries—26.1 and 25.8, respectively, per 1,000 marriages. After that the rate decreases for each additional year married, and by the fortieth anniversary, only 1.19 divorces occur per 1,000 marriages. Dr. Anne-Marie Ambert, *Divorce: Facts, Causes & Consequences*, November 2009. Report for the Vanier Institute of the Family, Ottawa.

15 Common-law unions have grown most rapidly among older age groups in recent years. The number of individuals aged 65 to 69 in common-law unions rose 66.5 per cent between 2006 and 2011, the fastest pace of all age groups. A. Milan, 2013. *Marital Status: Overview, 2011.* Statistics Canada Catalogue no. 91-209-X. Ottawa, Ontario. Report on the Demographic Situation in Canada.

16 McCarthy and McCarthy, *Therapy with Men after Sixty*, p. 32.

17 Prasso, *The Asian Mystique*, p. 191.

18 For example, the following study found that partners in happy marriages had significantly lower blood pressure compared with singles, even those with a network of social support. See J. Holt-Lunstad, et al., "Is there something unique about marriage? The relative impact of marital status, relationship quality, and network social support on ambulatory blood pressure and mental health," *Annals of Behavioral Medicine*; 35, no. 2 (April 2008): 239–244.

19 McCarthy and McCarthy, *Therapy with Men after Sixty*, p. 44.

20 The findings of the longitudinal study are discussed in George Vaillant's book *Aging Well* (New York: Little, Brown and Company, 2003).

21   Mary Elizabeth Hughes and Linda J. Waite, "Marital biography and health at mid-life," *Journal of Health and Social Behavior* 50, no. 3 (2009): 344–358.

22   S. Damaske, J. M. Smyth and M. J. Zawadzki (2014), "Has work replaced home as a haven? Re-examining Arlie Hochschild's time bind proposition with objective stress data," *Social Science & Medicine*, 115, 130–138.

23   Michelle Rotermann, "Marital breakdown and subsequent depression," *Health Reports* 18, no. 2 (May 2007), Statistics Canada, Ottawa, Catalogue 82-003.

24   "Isolation: The emerging crisis for older men," UK International Longevity Centre, 2014, http://www.independentage.org/media/828364/isolation-the-emerging-crisis-for-older-men-report.pdf.

25   Roger Angell, "This Old Man," *New Yorker*, February 17, 2014.

26   Tara Parker-Pope, "Divorce, it seems, can make you ill," *New York Times*, August 4, 2009.

27   The concept of our emotional circle was developed in *You Could Live a Long Time: Are You Ready?* and includes friends and family, as well as one's partner.

28   Margot and Laurent Martel, "Healthy living among seniors," supplement to *Health Reports*, Volume 16, Statistics Canada, Catalogue 82-003.

29   Jessica Allen, *Older People and Wellbeing*, Institute for Public Policy Research, July 2008, p. 27.

30   Michael Evans, "Social threads are tied to your well-being," *Globe and Mail*, November 27, 2007.

Relationship with Yourself

1   Bronfman, *The Third Act*, p. 81.

2   Jack Kerouac, *On the Road* (New York: Penguin Classics, 2003), p. viii.

3   John Leland, *Why Kerouac Matters: The Lessons of On the Road (They're Not What You Think)* (New York: Viking, 2007), p. 5.

4   Ibid., p. 45.

5   Ibid., p. 17.

6   Ibid., p. 6.

7   Ibid., p. 183.

8   Kerouac, *On the Road*, p. 106.

9   Simmons, *I'm Your Man*, p. 379.

10   Ibid., p. 406.

11   Martin Turcotte and Grant Schellenberg, *A Portrait of Seniors in Canada*, Statistics Canada, 2006, p. 211.

12   Jessica Allen, *Older People and Wellbeing*, Institute for Public Policy Research, July 2008, p. 36.

13   Corina R. Ronneberg, Edward Alan Miller, Elizabeth Dugan and Frank Porell, "The protective effects of religiosity on depression: A 2-year prospective study," *The Gerontologist*, June 2014.

14   For example, a controlled experiment reported in the *Journal of Environmental Psychology* involved 112 young adults who carried out stressful activities. "Sitting in a room with tree views promoted more rapid decline in diastolic blood pressure than sitting in a viewless room. Subsequently walking in a nature reserve initially fostered blood pressure change that indicated greater stress reduction than afforded by walking in urban surroundings" (http://aliveltd.org/rspace/nature.html). The Restorative Spaces website (http://aliveltd.org/rspace/index.html) talks about a variety of techniques to incorporate into a restorative practice and emphasizes the importance of taking time for self-care. The website grew out of a project to provide hospital nurses with a virtual lounge where they could go during the workday to have some self-care that went beyond just putting their feet up.

15   Jean Vanier, *Becoming Human* (Toronto: House of Anansi, 1998), p. 163.

16   The study looked at people aged 60 to 86. L. Fried, M. C. Carlson, M. Freedman, K. D. Frick, T. A. Glass, J. Hill, S. McGill, G. W. Rebok, T. Seeman, J. Tielsch, B. A. Wasik and S. Zeger. "A social model for health promotion for an aging population: Initial evidence on the Experience Corps model," *Journal of Urban Health* 1 (2004): 64–78, and Michelle C. Carlson et al., "Evidence for

neurocognitive plasticity in at-risk older adults: The Experience Corps Program," *The Journals of Gerontology Series A: Biological Sciences and Medical Sciences* 64, no. 12 (2009): 1275–1282.

17   S. J. Egger and B. H. Hensley, "Empowering spirituality and generativity through intergenerational connections," *Journal of Religion, Spirituality and Aging* 17, no. 1/2 (2005): 87–108.

18   Klein, *Travels with Epicurus*, p. 13.

19   Ibid., p. 15.

20   Michael Simmons, "Golden oldies," *Guardian*, September 27, 2000, http://www.theguardian.com/society/2000/sep/27/guardiansocietysupplement.

Conclusion

1   Richard J. Leider and David A. Shapiro, *Something to Live For: Finding Your Way in the Second Half of Life* (San Francisco: Berrett-Koehler Publishers, 2008), p. 19.

2   Ibid., p. 14.

3   Nikos Kazantzakis, *Zorba the Greek* (London: Faber and Faber, 1952),p. 165.

Suggestions for
Further Reading

———◆•◆•◆———

Retirement/Work

Encore: Finding Work That Matters in the Second Half of Life
by Marc Freedman (New York: Public Affairs, 2008)

Marc Freedman is the founder of Civic Ventures and
co-founder of the Purpose Prize and Experience Corps.
The *New York Times* calls him "the voice of aging baby
boomers [seeking] meaningful and sustaining work later
in life." The book tells the stories of men and women who
are searching for a calling in the second half of life. They
want work that offers continued income as well as meaning,
and a chance to do work that means something beyond
themselves. The US case studies include a businesswoman
who left a thirty-year career in the private sector to return
to her hometown and work with the public school system, a
car salesman who became a social entrepreneur and started
a non-profit organization to provide low-interest loans and

fuel-efficient cars to rural people of limited income, and a health care executive who became an advocate for the homeless. The book includes pointers to help you find your own encore career. Although the resources and examples are US-based, they offer valuable food for thought.

It's Your Time: Information and Exercises to Get You Ready for a Great Retirement by Donna McCaw (Toronto: BPS Books, 2011)

Donna McCaw is a Canadian retirement consultant who helps people prepare for their retirement years. Her book provides exercises and discussions for every stage of retirement planning. She begins with getting started and the emotional issues of moving away from the world of work. She reviews your financial needs in retirement, including the financial considerations of health care. A section on health and wellness looks at the top health issues affecting men and women, and how to prevent or manage them. The discussion on leisure helps you understand your leisure style, whether passive or active, and explores the value of volunteering. Relationships are addressed as well as the importance of keeping in touch with family and friends. There are checklists and resources to help you pull it all together.

Retire Retirement: Career Strategies for the Boomer Generation by Tamara Erickson (Boston: Harvard Business Press, 2008)

Tamara Erickson has researched changing demographics and how successful organizations work, and her book is about making choices and developing a career strategy for the rest of your life. The book discusses how to negotiate the best work environment, how to work with different generations, and how to create opportunities for yourself. The core work options are explored, either staying where you are but substantially renegotiating the terms of your work relationship, or doing something new and using the gift of time for reinvention. The book helps with developing personal strategies by exploring questions such as: *How much engagement do I want? What kind of work environment appeals to me? What level of compensation do I need? What kind of worker am I?*

The Joy of Not Working: A Book for the Retired, Unemployed, and Overworked by Ernie J. Zelinski (Toronto: Ten Speed Press, 2003)

As the title says, this book is for people at any stage of life about how to make the most of not working and enjoying life more. Ernie J. Zelinski is an Edmonton-based author with an engineering degree and an M.B.A. At the age of 29, he lost his job and never returned to traditional work.

People were always asking him why he wasn't bored, so he wrote this book to help people learn how to enjoy their leisure and fill their spare time with constructive and interesting activities. The book includes exercises, cartoons, diagrams and quotes. It was first published in 1997, and this current edition includes letters from people who read his first edition and made some life changes. Zelinski's message is to get a well-balanced life and not rely on your job to define who you are.

You Could Live a Long Time: Are You Ready? by **Lyndsay Green (Toronto: Dundurn Press, 2010)**

For this book I interviewed forty seniors aged 75 to 100 and asked them what I should be doing to live well at their age. These men and women from across Canada had been identified as role models, and they share their wisdom and strategies for independent and happy living. The book combines their advice with research to arrive at specific suggestions for what we should be doing now to prepare for old age, and includes resources to help implement the advice. Their message is that to get as much as possible out of my later years, I should embrace old age rather than trying to do the impossible to stay forever young. CBC's Peter Mansbridge says this about the book: "If you're betting you are going to be part of the live-longer and live-better crowd—and let's be frank, we all want to be—then whether you're twenty, sixty or anywhere in between you better read this book. It's full of advice, really good advice, that you'll be grateful you took when you hit those golden plus years."

YoungRetired.ca

This online video Web magazine provides resources for Canadians who are planning retirement. The website is provided by Charles Feaver, himself a young retiree based in Winnipeg. He offers short videos about topics such as making the transition to retirement, volunteering, work, health and fitness, lifelong learning, travel and more. The purpose of the website is to help Canadians on either side of the threshold of retirement plan how to enjoy their newly found freedom. Videos include those focused on "volun-tourism" with Cross-Cultural Solutions, an international non-profit organization providing volunteer opportunities around the world; ThirdQuarter.ca, which connects older workers with a variety of job openings; volunteering with Cuso International; becoming a part-time professor and touring Asia by bicycle.

FullyAlive65.com

Peter Bouffard's website offers support to men 50–plus so that they can live more fully after leaving their careers. The site features personal stories and lessons learned from men who are on their retirement path, as well as insights from experts. In addition to Peter's personal reflections, the site recommends resources including books and online links. Peter describes his life changing when he took up painting at age 50. Now 65, he expects to be retired within three years, and says he has been exposed to all of the retirement savings pitches over the years. He has grown more and more frustrated, knowing that financial wealth is not the only factor that needs to be considered. His hope is that his website will inspire men to make conscious choices to be fully alive in their retirement.

Finances

Redefining Retirement: New Realities for Boomer Women **by Margaret Hovanec and Elizabeth Shilton (Toronto: Second Story Press, 2007)**

The authors' goal is to help us develop a sustainable life-style for our retirement years, and, despite the book's title and focus, the advice is equally relevant to men. The book walks us through the construction of a Lifestyle Maintenance Budget to help us balance our income and expenditures after retirement. Exercises of cost-cutting and income-boosting help eliminate the gap between projected income and projected expenses. Tools include a monthly budget sheet with spending categories and practical tips for saving money. What sets this book apart is that Hovanec is a psychologist, and she understands our attachment to the glittering things money can buy. She reminds us before we make a purchase to calculate the amount of life energy the item cost. Life energy is the time we've spent in acquiring the money that we intend to trade for the product or service. The book's consistent message is that we have choices, and we should be making them.

Retirement's Harsh New Realities: Protecting Your Money in a Changing World by **Gordon Pape** (Toronto: Penguin Canada, 2012)

Gordon Pape is a sage Canadian financial planning expert, and this book lays out his tips for the essential steps for financial planning for retirement. Pape outlines how the global economic environment is changing and why we need to accept responsibility for our financial security. He sets out a number of harsh realities but provides workable solutions to each problem. There are sections on knowing your pension plan, building an RRSP, opening a TFSA, finding a dependable advisor and minimizing taxes. The book includes a personal lifestyle planner, a detailed worksheet to help people estimate their annual expenses and a table that allows you to factor in inflation. A valuable section of the book focuses on Pape's answers to the retirement questions that people have posed to him.

The Real Retirement: Why You Could Be Better Off Than You Think, and How to Make That Happen by Fred Vettese and Bill Morneau (Mississauga: John Wiley & Sons Canada, 2013)

Fred Vettese and Bill Morneau are retirement advisors, and their book explains how to set realistic retirement goals and offers concrete ways to achieve a comfortable retirement. They argue that Canadians not only can but, for the most part, will achieve a comfortable retirement. However, to reach their goals they will have to rely on personal responsibility for saving and investing for retirement. As mentioned, according to Vettese and Morneau, you need to replace about 50 per cent of your pre-retirement income to maintain your lifestyle. Their book catalogues post-retirement expenditures, breaking retirement down into three phases with very different financial requirements and emphasizing that consumption declines with advanced age. Phase 1 of retirement is the active age of retirement when expenses are at their highest to support goals people didn't have time for in their career. In Phase 2 people cut back on travel and other strenuous activities as their physical and/or mental capacities diminish. The majority of those who reach Phase 3 are in a nursing home, and most of these costs, at this point anyway, are covered by our national healthcare system.

Voluntary Simplicity: Toward a Way of Life That Is Outwardly Simple, Inwardly Rich (second revised edition) by Duane Elgin (New York: HarperCollins, 2010)

Duane Elgin is a former senior social scientist at the Stanford Research Institute, and he first published this book in 1981. The book's message about sustainable living has continued to speak to generations, and Elgin has continued to revise and update the book. Spending time reading this book helps us get at the roots of our desire to accumulate. Elgin's goal is to help us develop a life that is outwardly simple and inwardly rich. He explores a philosophy of simplicity that includes appreciating life and living more voluntarily (i.e., acting in a self-determining manner). He says that living a life of conscious simplicity will result in more balanced consumption, and he includes a set of consumption criteria to help us get at the root of why we buy what we do. Elgin's tenets of voluntary simplicity are frugal consumption, ecological awareness and personal growth, and the book describes the changes that an increasing number of Americans are making in their day-to-day living that are active, positive attempts to live simply. Elgin's goal is to help people change their lives and, in the process, save our planet.

Health

Being Mortal: Medicine and What Matters in the End by Atul Gawande (Toronto: Doubleday Canada, 2014)

Atul Gawande is a surgeon and bestselling author. His book uses research and case studies to explain how we have medicalized aging, frailty and death. Gawande argues for living to the last with autonomy, dignity and joy, which means accepting the limitations of medicine. The book focuses on the end of life and explores the roles of the hospice, the geriatrician and nursing home reformers. The book has important messages for anyone making decisions on medical treatments. By focusing on end of life, it reminds us to live consciously and fully, no matter what our stage in life.

"Change Your Mindset, Change the Game," TEDx talk given by Dr. Alia Crum, http://tedxtalks.ted. com/video/Change-Your-Mindset-Change-the (June 18, 2014)

Dr. Crum is a professor of psychology at Stanford University and a researcher who investigates how mindsets affect health and behaviour. Her research focuses on how changes in subjective mindsets—the lenses through which information is perceived, organized and interpreted—can alter objective reality through behavioural, psychological and physiological mechanisms. She is interested in understanding how mindsets affect outcomes outside the realm of medicine, including in the domains of behavioural health and organizational behaviour. Crum says the biggest game changer is "You—by harnessing the power of your mind."

Sexuality in Midlife and Beyond (Boston: The Harvard Health Publications, 2013), https://www.health.harvard. edu/special_health_reports/sexuality_in_midlife_and_ beyond

This report discusses the physical changes that come with age that affect sexuality, and talks about medications and health conditions (including diabetes, high blood pressure, heart disease and arthritis) that can create sexual difficulties. Declining hormone levels and changes in neurological and circulatory functioning may lead to sexual problems such as erectile dysfunction. But the emotional byproducts of maturity—increased confidence, better communication skills and lessened inhibitions—can help create a richer, more nuanced, and ultimately satisfying sexual experience. The advice in this report applies broadly to people of all sexual orientations. The report includes treatments, medications and self-help techniques that can resolve common sexual problems.

The Brain That Changes Itself (New York: Viking, 2007) and *The Brain's Way of Healing* (New York: Viking, 2015) by Norman Doidge, M.D.

Dr. Norman Doidge is a psychiatrist and a psychoanalyst. His books document research from the frontiers of neuro-plasticity—the idea that the brain can change its own structure and function through thought and activity. The books use a combination of research findings and case studies to explore the implications of the changing brain for understanding love, sexual attraction, taste, culture and education. Doidge explains that our brains are not only more resourceful but also more vulnerable to outside influences. Neuroplasticity has the power to produce more flexible but also more rigid behaviours, a phenomenon Doidge calls "the plastic paradox." Doidge hopes that by understanding both the positive and negative effects of plasticity we can truly understand the extent of human possibilities.

Younger Next Year: Live Strong, Fit, and Sexy—Until You're 80 and Beyond by Chris Crowley and Henry (Harry) S. Lodge (New York: Workman Publishing Co., 2007)

This book is written to persuade men to take charge of their health and draws on the science of aging to show how men 50 or older can become functionally younger, enjoy life and be stronger, healthier and more alert. The program is set out in a series of "Harry's Rules." One of the men I interviewed said that Harry was his role model. "I really try to block off at least an hour a day to go out and get exercise," Murray said. "It was *Younger Next Year* that gave me my prescription for this. Harry emphasizes the importance of making exercise fun and to buy something nice if you have to encourage yourself. This is how I rationalize going on my extended road trips with the biking club." Here's Harry's General Rule of Gear: "It's not that easy just to get out of bed in the morning and train, six days a week. So, if you're doing it, you deserve decent gear. Skimp on washing machines and junk like that. Buy good gear."

Subliminal: How Your Unconscious Mind Rules Your Behavior **by Leonard Mlodinow (Toronto: Vintage Books, 2013)**

Leonard Mlodinow has a Ph.D. in theoretical physics and teaches at the California Institute of Technology. His previous books include *The Grand Design*, which he co-authored with Stephen Hawking. This book reviews the latest scientific research on the power of the unconscious mind to change our view of ourselves and the world around us. Mlodinow explores many aspects of the unconscious mind's influence: how we misperceive our relationships with family, friends and business associates; how we misunderstand the reasons for our investment decisions; and how we misremember important events. The unconscious aspects of human behaviour were actively speculated about by Jung, Freud and many others over the past century, but new technologies have revolutionized our understanding of the part of the brain that operates below our conscious mind. Mlodinow explains this new development of a science of the unconscious.

Civic Engagement

The Catholic Immigration Centre has prepared a resource for potential volunteers called *Attention Boomers: Change the World . . . Again! A Toolkit to Meaningful Volunteering*. The document offers examples of ways to volunteer and techniques for finding volunteer activities. There are good tips on finding the right volunteer fit, including a list of questions that focus on the volunteer's values and areas of interest and goals. The document can be downloaded from the website at http://www.cic.ca/50plus/Boomer Volunteer Toolkit EN.pdf.

The website of Volunteer Canada (Volunteer.ca) has a section called "I Want to Volunteer." They work with over 200 volunteer centres nationwide that facilitate connections between people and volunteer opportunities. The website also has an online tool for volunteer matching.

VolunteerMatch (VolunteerMatch.org) is a US website that matches volunteer jobs with volunteers. Even though you won't be able to use their services to find a volunteer position in Canada, you can find virtual volunteer opportunities. Their website is worth exploring because of its many examples of volunteerism.

Relationships with Others

Getting the Love You Want: 20th Anniversary Edition: A Guide for Couples by Harville Hendrix (New York: Holt Paperbacks, 2007)

This book was originally published in 1988 and is based on Imago relationship therapy, a process developed by husband and wife team Harville Hendrix and Helen LaKelly Hunt, who are educators and therapists. Imago therapy explores the connections between the frustrations experienced in adult relationships and early childhood experiences. The goal is to move from blaming your partner and being reactive, to developing understanding and empathy. The goal is to transform conflicts into opportunities for healing and growth, and help partners connect more deeply and lovingly. The book has a workbook and study guide. Mental health professionals trained in the Imago method offer face-to-face relationships and couple therapy. More information is available on the Imago website at ImagoRelationships.org. While I have not personally participated in an Imago workshop, therapists I know and respect have found the process to be successful with their clients.

The Creative Age: Awakening Human Potential in the Second Half of Life by Gene D. Cohen, M.D. (New York: Quill, 2001)

As mentioned, the late Dr. Gene Cohen was a geriatric psychiatrist who spent decades studying people over 60 years of age and helping them get more out of their later years. This book debunks harmful myths about aging and explores the biological and emotional foundations of creativity. Cohen describes how the unique combination of age, experience and creativity can produce inner growth and expand potential. The book interweaves history, scientific research, stories and Cohen's own insights. Cohen stresses that life is a work in progress, and the book includes strategies for incorporating creativity into everyday activities. He emphasizes building a Social Portfolio and identifying new opportunities for creativity through new and existing relationships. The book contains a step-by-step activity plan for strengthening your relationship with your partner. The approach is based on a technique called collaborative creativity, which is intended to deepen your emotional intimacy and connectedness.

Relationship with Yourself

Becoming Human by Jean Vanier (Toronto: House of Anansi, 2008)

This book is based on Jean Vanier's CBC Massey Lecture Series. Vanier is the Catholic philosopher, theologian and humanitarian who founded l'Arche, an international organization of communities for the developmentally disabled. Vanier calls on us to open ourselves to those we perceive as different or inferior. This, he says, is the key to true personal and societal freedom. By embracing weakness, we learn new ways of living and discover greater compassion, trust and understanding. This spirit of inclusion has extraordinary implications for the way we live our lives and build our communities.

Care of the Soul: A Guide for Cultivating Depth and Sacredness in Everyday Life by Thomas Moore (New York: HarperCollins, 1994)

Thomas Moore has degrees in theology, musicology and philosophy, and lived as a monk in a Catholic religious order for twelve years. He writes in the areas of archetypal psychology, mythology and the imagination. This book is Moore's personal statement based on his experience as a psychotherapist, coupled with insights from people through the ages who have written about the nature and needs of the soul. Moore believes that by caring for the soul we can find relief from our distress and discover deep satisfaction and pleasure. He says the soul is revealed in attachment, love and community, as well as in retreat on behalf of inner communing and intimacy. Caring for the soul isn't about perfection or even improvement, and doesn't look for a trouble-free existence. Rather it is an appreciation of the paradoxical mysteries that blend light and darkness into the grandeur of what human life and culture can be.

How Rembrandt Reveals Your Beautiful, Imperfect Self **by Roger Housden (New York: Random House, 2005)**

Poet and writer Roger Housden uses the example of Rembrandt's life and work as inspiration for the strength we need to live with passion and an unflinching acceptance of who we are. The book is part biography, part history, part art appreciation. Housden shows how the incredible life and work of Rembrandt can serve as a wise and honest mirror to clarify our own hopes, struggles and aspirations. The book explores six lessons that draw on Rembrandt's self-portraits and life story: Open your eyes; Love this world; Troubles will come; Stand like a tree; Keep the faith; Embrace the inevitable.

(Images of Rembrandt's self-portraits can be found at the Web Museum at Ibiblio.org.)

Transitions: Making Sense of Life's Changes (twenty-fifth anniversary edition) by William Bridges (Cambridge: Da Capo Press, 2004)

William Bridges is a management consultant who first published *Transitions* in 1980. This was one of the first books to explore the underlying pattern of transition and was named one of the fifty most important self-help books of all time. As mentioned, the book is a guide for coping with the inevitable changes in life and takes readers step-by-step through the three stages of transition: the ending, the neutral zone and the new beginning. The book offers a road map for navigating change and moving into a hopeful future. When I interviewed Albert, he told me that he had read and enjoyed Bridges's earlier books but felt that *Transitions* stood out. "Bridges himself faced a transitional time involving the death of a much loved spouse," Albert said. "Previously he had understood the steps of transitions at an academic level, but had never experienced them on such a personal and intimate level. This loss bears some similarities to the experience of those who are forced into retirement."

Travels with Epicurus: A Journey to a Greek Island in Search of a Fulfilled Life by Daniel Klein (New York: Penguin Books, 2012)

When author Daniel Klein was in his 70s he went to the Greek island Hydra to see whether the philosopher Epicurus could teach him about the pleasures available only late in life.

The book draws on the inspiring lives of his Greek friends as well as philosophers ranging from Epicurus to Sartre. The resulting book is a travel book, a witty and accessible meditation, and an optimistic guide to living well. This is a pilgrimage into those refined pleasures that maybe only a mature mind can fully appreciate. Pleasures such as the auto-biographical imperative—the fundamental task at this stage to reflect back on one's life, and the enjoyment from pondering transcendent questions such as the meaning of it all.

Understanding Men's Passages: Discovering the New Map of Men's Lives by Gail Sheehy (New York: Random House, 1998)

Gail Sheehy, the author of *Passages*, has been chronicling social trends for decades. As mentioned, this book is the first time she singled out men. For her research Sheehy spoke to hundreds of men over the age of 40 to discuss the turbulent challenges and surprising pleasures they found in midlife. The book explores work anxieties, concerns over sexual potency, marital and family stress, and issues of power. It is organized by decades, and the men share their desires, fears and cravings for renewal. They are looking for new passion and purpose to invigorate the second half of their lives, dealing with "manopause," surviving job change, enjoying post-nesting zest, facing depression and trying to figure out what keeps a man young.